# G O D

## EXPLAINED

# GOD

## EXPLAINED

Leaders from Thirty Different Religions Interpret God

# Miles Barnett

# GOD EXPLAINED
## LEADERS FROM THIRTY DIFFERENT RELIGIONS INTERPRET GOD

*Scripture quotations marked NIV are taken from the Holy Bible, New International Version®. NIV®. Copyright © 1973, 1978, 1984 by International Bible Society. Used by permission of Zondervan. All rights reserved. [Biblica]*

*iUniverse books may be ordered through booksellers or by contacting:*

*iUniverse*
*1663 Liberty Drive*
*Bloomington, IN 47403*
*www.iuniverse.com*
*1-800-Authors (1-800-288-4677)*

*ISBN: 978-1-4917-9466-1 (sc)*
*ISBN: 978-1-4917-9465-4 (e)*

*Library of Congress Control Number: 2016906748*

*Print information available on the last page.*

*iUniverse rev. date: 01/12/2017*

When I first had the idea for this book, I mentioned it to a number of people. The majority told me it could not be done, because God could never be defined. A few not only liked the idea but offered to assist me on my quest. After several months, the few who liked the idea became many. I offer my gratitude to all those who helped create this book.

I would like to thank Ray Sypniewski, Steve Spreitzer, Avinash and Sema Shah, Mark Liss, Jay Reinheimer, and Edward Cherkinsky for all their support and encouragement. I especially thank my wife, Deborah, for tolerating me while I was working on this project.

# Contents

# Introduction

I started this book with a very simple idea: I would ask leaders of different religious groups to define their God, thinking they would do it joyfully, since they discuss this entity every day of their lives. I was a fool to think it would be that simple.

The idea came about because of religious prejudice I'd observed having worked as an educator for more than thirty-five years. It always bewildered me that people who should be highly educated would make disparaging remarks about religion, race, and sexual preference. These same individuals, after making discriminatory remarks, continually mentioned some form of God's will. I was never sure what God they were talking about, since they also mentioned how their God was kind, loving, caring, and forgiving. The purpose of this book is to help people understand that others may have a different comprehension of God or not believe there is a God and that these unique views are different, not right or wrong.

In order to explain how people perceived God, I asked leaders from thirty different religious groups to explain their perceptions of God. My thought was, if people can have a better understanding of the different views of God, it may lead to an open dialogue, allowing for better religious understanding. It may also give individuals perceptions into their own religions and have them become more involved in their belief systems.

The religious leaders who participated gave me essays, sermons, letters, liturgies, and interviews about their belief or lack of belief in God. A number of the participants wrote or spoke from the heart, while some only quoted from their religious texts and never explained their views of God. Others did as little as possible, neither giving extensive quotes from their religious texts nor explaining their views of God.

I have also included overviews of the religious groups that have contributed to this book. The overviews are intended to give readers some insight into the background and beliefs of each religion presented. They do not tell everything about the religions; readers who are interested in learning more about specific religions can research them independently.

The beginning of this book starts with the atheist point of view. The atheists are outliers of religious thought yet one of the few groups that stated emphatically that people should be able to practice their own religions. They stated that religious individuals should not force others to participate in a thought that was not of their own choosing.

# *Atheist*

The atheist movement was started by Madalyn Murray O'Hair when she filed a lawsuit to allow her son not to be forced to attend Bible readings in his school. The original suit was consolidated into *Abington School District v. Schemp*. The case was based on the First Amendment, part of the Bill of Rights, which states, "Congress shall make no law respecting an establishment of religion or prohibiting the free exercise thereof; or abridging the freedom of speech, of the press; or the right of the people peaceably to assemble, or petition the Government for redress of grievances." The Supreme Court ruled in 1963 that enforcement of sanctioned and organized Bible reading in a public school system is unconstitutional. Madalyn Murray O'Hair went on to found the American Atheists organization, which advocates for the separation of church and state.

## Finding a Spokesperson

I called the Michigan Atheist Organization and talked to Arlene-Marie, the director of the organization. She invited me to her home, where we sat on the back porch, had coffee, and talked about her experiences. Arlene is a very nice, bright, beautiful, and driven person who believes strongly in the rights of the atheists. Arlene was friends with Madalyn Murray O'Hair (the founder of the atheist movement) and has been an atheist activist for more than forty years. In 2011 the organization she directs was named the number-one local atheist group in the country. Arlene has been interviewed on numerous radio and television talk shows. She has been invited to many universities and schools to share her point of view. Arlene has appeared in a panel discussion with Richard Dawkins; spoken before the National Press Club in Washington, DC; and presented on the National Mall in DC and on the steps of the US Supreme Court. She has also been involved in numerous activities for the American Atheists organization and has received many accolades for her work. The following is taken directly from speeches that Arlene-Marie has given at numerous events. I am sorry to say that Arlene-Marie passed before this book was published.

## By Arlene-Marie

The American Religious Identification Survey reports that the godless community is among the largest and fastest-growing groups in the country. One out of every five Americans is godless. It's a number that keeps growing daily. Many of these people are atheist.

Who are the atheists? We are those who do not accept humanity's claims of gods—be it Jehovah, Allah, Vishnu, Zeus, or any of the additional gods worshipped today. Atheism is not a belief. It is a conclusion based on lack of evidence. We do not hate God or worship the devil. That would be impossible, as we don't accept claims of their existence.

Where do we find these millions of atheists? We are not easy to spot; we don't look alike, dress alike, or have specific cultures or traditions. The only thing we have in common is that we live our lives free of the dogmas of traditional theology. We are your neighbors, coworkers, friends, or family members. We're doctors, lawyers, merchants, teachers, students, and military and law-enforcement personnel. In other words, we are found in every walk of life—including the ministry.

In a survey by Linda LaScola and Daniel Dennett titled "Preachers Who Are Not Believers," it was pointed out that a number of religious leaders no longer believed in what they have been taught.

Because of this survey, Richard Dawkins, Daniel Dennett, Linda LaScola, and former minister Dan Barker started the Clergy Project. This project provides a safe house community for current and former ministers who no longer hold the supernatural beliefs of their religious tradition. Currently members may join this project by invitation only.

Some have claimed that because atheists do not accept belief in God, they have no morals. We break morality into two parts: basic morality and cultural morality. The rules of basic morality deal with murder, theft, and lying. The cultural rules of morality dictate what worship practices one must or must not engage in, what sexual and reproductive practices one must or must not engage in, what items of clothing and jewelry one must or must not wear, what foods one must or must not eat, what days one must or must not work, who may marry and who may not, gender rules designed to keep women in their place, what is and is not a sin, and who may or may not go to heaven or hell. There are many more cultural rules than the ones mentioned. Atheists recognize the value and need for the basic rules of morality. We feel justified in rejecting the cultural moral codes, as they are laced with the dogmas of traditional theologies. Instead, we strive to seek an ethical philosophy of daily life that has the most tangible and rational foundation possible. We know that theocratic power is reduced when people learn to tell the difference between basic morality and cultural morality.

Many people claim that America is a Christian nation, with the Ten Commandments being the building block for our legal system. We are not a Christian nation. We are governed by a secular document, the US Constitution, which contains no mention of God or Christianity. Its only references to religion are exclusionary, such as in Article VI, which states, "No religious test shall be required as qualification to any office of public trust." In the First Amendment is the statement "Congress shall make no law respecting an establishment of religion, or prohibiting the free exercise thereof." American law is not based on the Ten Commandments; it is based on British common law. The Ten Commandments are based on religious theology.

What are the atheists up to? Most atheists are simply busy getting on with the chores and joys of daily life. But thousands more are busy protecting their civil rights. We know that freedom is the distance between state and church, and we are busy defending freedom *from* religion and freedom *of* religion. We struggle daily to keep the wall that separates state and church from falling into the hands of religious extremists. This is our mission.

# Anglican Church

In schools, students were taught that "the Anglican Church is the Church of England which severed allegiance to the papacy during the Protestant Reformation."[1] In religious terms, it was thought of as the midway point between Protestantism and Roman Catholicism. The Anglican Church of North America was founded in 1977 at a religious conclave held in Saint Louis, Missouri. This convention was made up of two hundred religious leaders who were against changes that were being made in the Episcopal Church, especially modifications that dealt with the ordination of women and revisions that were being made to the prayer book.

## Finding a Spokesperson

Father Greg McComas and I met at the church for which he is assistant pastor. We went into the meeting hall and sat at a table, at which time I presented the concept for this book. Father Greg told me that something like this was tried before—not as a book but as gatherings between Catholic groups to discuss their views. It appeared that these meetings did not work out well. He then reflected on whether to become part of this project. After a few phone calls and meetings, he decided to add his thoughts about God to this undertaking. The following is Father Greg McComas's essay.

---

[1] Frank S. Mead and Samuel S. Hill, *Handbook of Denominations in the United States 11th Edition*, revised by Craig D. Atwood (Nashville: Abington Press, 2001), 129.

# Jesus as the Best Reflection of God

## By Father Greg McComas

Foundationally, God is one who can make truth known and bring order to chaos. This concept of God as a God of order did not come to me easily, as I fancied myself an iconoclast growing up, inspired to knock others out of their comfort zones. I suppose I was successful, to some extent, if alienating others is a yardstick! Anyway, while I still love innovative ideas in regard to communication and the practice of one's faith, I am now rather suspicious of novel ideas about who God is. I'm one who is inclined to stick with the ancient Christian faith; thus, where I come across in this composition as perhaps *too* confident in my beliefs, my prayer is that I'm only reflecting what God has broadly and plainly made known and not anything unique that I've come up with on my own. I would like to be a person who is both very flexible regarding true mysteries of the divine and yet faithful not to contradict God's trustworthy revelation in the Bible.

I see God predominantly in the face of Jesus. I see the face of Jesus most clearly in the holy scriptures, which are about him, from beginning to end (the New Testament). In this world of subjective, ever-changing knowledge, there is no hope that people can come to know objective, unchanging, transcendent truth from their own experience or cultural history—unless, that is, God breaks into our own subjective realm with his objective revelation. And that is what I believe he has done with Jesus and the written word of God.

People—who are made in the image of God—reflect God in many ways too; I see, and try to see (as C. S. Lewis said), the weight of glory that people bear and may one day fully bear. This vision of the stained yet expectant glory of humans gives some content to my perception of God but still remains in the realm of the subjective. That is why we all needed Jesus to come into our world—our human realm. (Having mentioned Lewis, also an Anglican, I would note that my view of God has been deeply influenced by his book *Mere Christianity*.)

Therefore I would say my view of God is not fundamentally academic—uniquely known through Bible study. It is also equally personal, experiential, and existential. I see myself as personally connected, known, and restored to God through Jesus. I accept that Jesus is God and is the door through which one may truly know the divine. Because of Jesus, I know God and am known; my sins are forgiven, my character made better, my sympathy and empathy—concern to help others with loving actions—grows, my soul is unconditionally loved, and my life given meaning and direction. Further, my eternal destiny is full of hope for life in God's presence that never ceases. And this does not end at the individual level. God is the one who wants peace for individuals, families, communities, and all the nations of earth.

## Other and Alike; Far and Near

God is the majestic "King of kings and Lord of lords" echoed in Handel's *Messiah*; he is not only king of all created life, energy, and substance, but Jesus is *my* king and *my* Lord.

He is unfathomably "other"—beyond my comprehension, ineffably awesome. And yet at the same time he is likewise personal, intimately present, indwelling. Although king, he has made me his adopted child, and to continue with Trinitarian language, God the Father is *my* Father; God the Son is *my* friend; God the Holy Spirit is *my* advocate.

This "profoundly other and yet deeply similar" paradigm dominates much of how I understand God. I see God as infinitely bigger than the universe—the creator and sustainer of all—and I see him as nearer and more integral to my environment and very being than all the atomic and subatomic forces within and without my physical presence. The E (energy) of $E = mc^2$ is thoroughly dependent on God but does not define him. God is Spirit, beyond physics (metaphysical), and he is physically present as well. The one who on one level is completely "other" has made humankind in his own image. We are like him, and as mentioned above, in many ways, we bear his glory.

God infuses my soul with life and meaning at every moment; he perfectly loves me, personally; he gives my life weight and significance that is lasting. Again, God is my Father, friend, and advocate. He even is the romancer of my soul, calling, indeed wooing me to return to him whenever I stray.

My Father in heaven is the one who hears my prayers and answers them. He is both Father and king of me personally, my family, and my spiritual family (the brotherhood of believers adopted into God's household, the church—imperfect as it is). He is my all in all. And so I see God as my guide, my protector, my life, my everything—whom I am to follow with joy, even when he guides me through difficulties and trials. Therefore I acknowledge God as good—all the time.

In summing up this thought, I sense that most people of faith are repulsed by the tenet that people are here only because of time plus chance; because if this were true, for example, there would be no moral difference between lopping off a tree branch and cutting off another person's arm. There would be no rational basis for morality at all, "since it's all time and chance, period." (Such logic has led even the influential philosopher Anthony Flew to convert from atheism to theism.) What I am trying to say is that God is not only "true enough" to be a foundation for morality; he is also *personal*—and amazingly so.

Trinitarian Essence

I alluded to God as Trinity a few paragraphs up. Although the word *Trinity* is not in scripture, we have to talk about God's complexity and unity *somehow*, in particular, how he revealed himself through scripture with language that affirms: God the Father is a person, the Holy Spirit is a person, and that of course Jesus is a person, each of whom is equated in various ways with affirmations of divinity. All the while, the testimony of scripture unwaveringly maintains that God is one. I see God, then, as consistent with the traditional biblical understanding of three-in-one and one-in-three.

From eternity past, God has existed in a manner of complexity-in-unity and unity-in-complexity. There was never a time when agape love (pure, unconditional love) did not exist, as it was always a part of the interior relation of the one triune Godhead.

That is, he did not need to create us to love; he already had love in himself.

Briefly, with great abbreviation, in scripture there are both subtle hints and strong affirmations of such complexity. I've learned the "royal" sense of *we* did not exist where God was recorded as saying, "Let us make man in our image ...," "Let us confound ...," "Who will go for us?" Therefore, when God says *us* of himself, there is a sense of complexity and not just speech akin to a modern unitary monarch. Moreover, "In the beginning," in Genesis 1, there is God the Father, the Word, and the Spirit, acting, creating as one. There is the dominant Hebrew word for God, *Elohim* as plural in form yet singular in essence. Predominantly, there is the divine personhood of Father, Son, and Spirit, referenced in many contexts, and to take just one New Testament example, there is the singular "Name" of the one God, per the Great Commission (Matthew 28), referencing the plural "the Father, the Son, and the Holy Spirit." Further examples abound.

Normally I would say that "I see God as Trinity" only very briefly in such a concise account as this, but since the modern mind and modern church tend to struggle seeing God as Trinity, I think it's helpful to continue for a bit to emphasize its significance. Why? Well, as the saying goes, in the beginning God created humankind in God's own image; ever since, we have been trying to return the favor, creating our view of God in *our* own image. Therefore, in these modern times, our "enlightened" minds tend to be hostile to the notion of "hierarchy and equality existing simultaneously in peace"—all because that doesn't fit the newer views of justice and morals. Nevertheless, there is indeed equality in the Godhead and also order—a hierarchy of roles (cf. the Athanasian Creed) but not of essence. And this harmony of equality and hierarchy (admittedly not easy to summarize) is a beautiful thing when in balance, both in heaven and on earth. God, though, is increasingly being renamed and rereferenced in accord with human desires, rather than as revealed in scripture. I'm trying to stick to the classic view, where Trinitarian order and hierarchy—and equality as well—exist in perfect accord. Therefore, although it is arguably not easy for Christians (or others) to understand the Godhead, nevertheless, the Trinity brings understanding to everything else in Christianity. There is beauty and goodness in the order of the Trinity, how creation was ordered, and there is beauty and goodness in the order of God's recreation of the church and of individuals.

## Concluding Reflection

I would say that I see God as not only real but much *more* real than we see ourselves—in the sense of the classic analogy that, compared to God, we presently live in a mere two-dimensional, grayscale land of shadows, whereas God naturally exists— unbounded by time or place or any constraint—and has his being in vibrant, multidimensional glory. To this glory he calls us. This is the very God who breaks through the subjective essence of our age and brings trustworthy revelation of himself through Jesus Christ—who, as the Bible says—loves us personally. And thus the unshakable good news is that in his love for you and me, Christ has died and has risen from the dead, and in his justice for all, he will come again to make all wrongs right.

Finally, because I see God as fundamentally loving and ever good without exception, he never would have allowed Jesus to die as a crucified sacrifice for us unless it was absolutely necessary for everyone. God is neither barbaric nor capricious, sending his Son to cruel death to simply create yet one more pathway to himself if many others already worked just fine. And God is not threatened when people disagree with him on this or anything else; he simply presses ahead with what is loving and just in perfect balance. He does not countenance crusades or pogroms of legalism or insecurity. He doesn't redefine justice to consolidate power, to put others down, or for any other reason. God does not manipulate or coerce our will in any way that denigrates our dignity and the genuine choices we make. And through it all, God wants his believers to mirror him in always extending such respectful love to others. The love and humility of Jesus go hand in hand, and God is the head who imparts his love and humility to his family. From eternity past to eternity future, God remains both the loving Father and the sovereign king.

# *Baha'i*

Baha'i is one of the smallest religions in the world. The religion does not consider itself to be a sect of Islam but a separate and distinct religion. The Baha'i believe that there have been nine great prophets in the world, all sent by God. The prophets were sent to teach man to become closer to God. The main belief in the Baha'i religion is to have the people of the world unite as one. Other beliefs are: there should be independent investigation of the truth, science and religion are harmonious, the sexes are equal, all economic problems have a spiritual solution, all prejudice should be eliminated, and there should be a universal auxiliary language. The Baha'i do not have a clergy but rely on unpaid teachers to help seekers of the religion.

## Finding a Spokesperson

Dianne wanted to make it clear that she was writing about her personal experience in the Baha'i faith and does not at all presume to speak for other Baha'is. I met Dianne by calling the national office. They directed me to her as a member of the Baha'i Area Teaching Committee. When we met, it was obvious that Dianne is a sincere, articulate, and kind person. I explained the purpose of my book, and she offered to help. Her essay follows.

## "O God, My God, My Beloved, My Heart's Desire"

### By Dianne Coin

My God is the God of Krishna and the Hindus, of Abraham, Moses, and the Jews: the God of Zoroaster, Buddha, Christ, and Muhammad. He is the source of the world's great religions.

God created all that exists and gave each thing one of his own qualities. Man, however, is special because God created him with the potential to reflect all of his qualities. But just as a painting or a sculpture cannot comprehend its maker, so too am I incapable of comprehending my God in his essential glory and power.

> O Son of Man! Veiled in My immemorial being and in the ancient eternity of my essence I knew my love for thee: therefore I created thee, have engraved on thee Mine image and revealed to thee My beauty. (*The Hidden Words of Baha'u'llah*, Arabic 3)

I am able to know God through his most recent messengers, the Bab and Baha'u'llah. With them God initiated a new, independent world religion — the Baha'i faith — and a new age in the evolution of religion. Muhammad, the prophet of Islam, was the last of God's prophet-messengers. In that cycle God's prophets foretold of a time on this earth when peace, prosperity, and unity would one day be achieved among all men.

With the Bab, Baha'u'llah, and the Baha'i faith, God begins a new cycle, in which prophecies of earlier religions will at last be fulfilled.

> He who is your Lord, the All-Merciful, cherished in His heart the desire of beholding the entire human race as one soul and one body. The fundamental purpose animating the Faith of God and His Religion is to safeguard the interests and promote

14

the unity of the human race, and to foster the spirit of love and fellowship amongst men … This is the straight Path, the fixed and unmovable foundation. (Gleanings from the writings of Baha'u'llah)

My God gives me clear guidance so that I may follow his straight path and fulfill my purpose to promote the unity of the human race. I can read his guidance in the most holy book, *The Kitab-i-Aqdas*, and in other holy writings like *The Hidden Words of Baha'u'llah*.

*The Hidden Words of Baha'u'llah* begins with this passage:

> This is that which hath descended from the realm of glory, uttered by the tongue of power and might, and revealed unto the Prophets of old. We have taken the inner essence thereof and clothed it in the garment of brevity, as token of grace unto the righteous, that they may stand faithful unto the Covenant of God, may fulfill in their lives His trust, and in the realm of spirit obtain the gem of Divine virtue.

While investigating the Baha'i faith, as part of my search for spiritual truth, I found God. This is the most important event in my life. It enables me to clearly understand my origin, my purpose, my destination, and the means for making ready.

> Truthfulness is the foundation of all human virtues. Without truthfulness progress and success in all the worlds of God are impossible for any soul. (Abdu'l-Baha, *The Advent of Divine Justice*)

> Do not be content with showing friendship in words alone, let your heart burn with loving-kindness for all who may cross your path. (Abdu'l-Baha, Paris talks)

O son of Being! How couldst thou forget thine own faults and busy thyself with the faults of others? Whoso doeth this is accursed of Me. (*The Hidden Words of Baha'u'llah*, Arabic 26)

There is nothing sweeter in the world of existence than prayer ... It creates spirituality, creates mindfulness and celestial feelings, begets new attractions of the Kingdom, and engenders the susceptibilities of the higher intelligence. (Abdu'l-Baha, *Star of the West*)

By simply setting aside for a brief moment my lifelong skepticism and allowing for the possibility that he might actually exist, I experienced the presence of God for the first time.

O son of Being! Love me, that I may love thee. If thou lovest Me not, my love can in no wise reach thee. Know this, O servant. (*The Hidden Words of Baha'u'llah*, Arabic 5)

God assures me that my heart is his home and that he is always with me. He assuages my fear and repairs it with confidence and certainty.

O son of Being! With the hands of Power I made thee and with the fingers of strength I created thee: and within thee have I placed the essence of My light. Be thou content with it and seek naught else, for My work is perfect and My command is binding. Question it not, nor have a doubt thereof. (*Hidden Words of Baha'u'llah*, Arabic 12)

## A Gift for You

O God! Refresh and gladden my spirit.
Purify my heart. Illumine my powers.

I Lay all my affairs in Thy hand. Thou art my Guide
and my Refuge. I will no longer be sorrowful and
grieved; I will be a happy and joyful being.

Oh God! I will no longer be full of anxiety, nor will I let trouble
harass me. I will not dwell on the unpleasant things of life.

Oh God! Thou art more friend to me than I am to
myself. I dedicate myself to Thee, O Lord.
—Abdu'l-Baha, Baha'i prayers

# *Baptist*

Baptists are "one of the largest and most diverse groupings of Christians in the United States."[2] Each church is independent. However, the churches are grouped into associations that usually have yearly conventions. There are certain principles that all Baptist churches follow: the lordship of Jesus Christ is established, the Bible is the sole rule of life, people have the freedom to approach God for themselves, and salvation is granted "through faith by the way of grace and contact with the Holy Spirit."[3] Baptists also believe in the unity of humankind, life after death, separation between church and state, and that God's kingdom will triumph over the world.

## Finding a Spokesperson

Pastor Good was one of the first people I met when I began this book. He invited me to meet with him in his office at the church in which he officiates. At that time I explained the reasons for writing this book. He listened intently and said he would join in on the project, but he wanted periodic updates about what I had learned. I dropped by his church for the next seven months with explanations of what I had discovered. Finally he stated that his sermon the following Sunday was about perseverance and that

---

[2] Frank S. Mean and Samuel S. Hill, *Handbook of Denominations in the United States 11th Edition*, Revised by Craig D. Atwood (Nashville: Abington Press, 2001), 42.

[3] Ibid.

19

he would send me his statement of faith. The following is Pastor Good's statement of faith.

## By Dr. Jon D. Good

The Christian faith has historically held the Bible, the church, and context as sources for authority. As a participant in the Christian faith, these sources serve as authority for my own faith and belief in God. My own context and experience with God are the windows through which I understand the Bible and the church. The church as a body of believers has a rich tradition that illuminates revelations of God and provides a community in which to understand these revelations. Additionally, the church body serves as a source of accountability for my faith and experience. The Bible as God's word is the primary source for my faith. It contains the most significant revelations of God and serves as a source of direction (Ephesians 6:17; James 1:21–23). Therefore, I describe and articulate my faith according to these sources of authority.

As my primary source of authority, the Bible sets up the framework through which I understand and articulate my theology. The Bible illuminates the events of God's disclosure as revelation by means of the narrative. It is the great story of God's actions toward humanity that begs to be told. The chapters in the story form a basic framework for the Christian faith, while it is the telling and living out of this story in the world that shows the real and relevant presence of God. This story, as the illumination of God's working, requires a particular place and time with a particular language and setting. The very nature of the story is to be told. When it is told, the illumination of God's revelation in this story brings to light the reality and working of God in a particular context with particular people. My own encounter with this story through my own context has brought to light God's desire for relationship with me and has inspired me to tell the story to others.

The first chapter presented by the Bible is that of God being the great creator and humanity as part of that creation. The creation is God's first act of love and relationship toward humanity. The sole purpose of this creation is to be in relations to God. God had no need or requirement to create; creation was primarily for the divine image (Genesis 1:27). There are four important elements to understanding how humanity is created in the image of God. The first element is that there is a clear distinction between humanity and the rest of creation. Even though humanity is part of creation, it is clearly fashioned in such a way that it is set apart from the whole of creation. This uniqueness becomes apparent in light of a special relationship we have with God the Creator. The fact that God is constantly involved in our lives through transformation, creation, and reconciliation alludes to this special relationship (Jeremiah 18:6; Philippians 3:21; Romans 8:28; 2 Corinthians 5:17). Moving beyond this distinction, we see the next element important to understanding how we are created in God's image: the soul (James 5:20; Luke 2:35). Having a spiritual nature that is like God gives humanity a special place in the sight of God. However, this special place of the human should be both a physical and spiritual existence. Humanity is created in God's image at both the physical and spiritual level. The next element is that God has trusted humanity with the care of creation (Genesis 1:17). Thus, with this privilege and freedom comes the sense of responsibility. Humanity is held accountable for the maintenance of the goodness of creation as well as the well-being of itself. The last element comes with the special relationship between God and humanity: the nature of response. Humanity is to respond to its Creator and seek out that special relationship offered by God (John 3:16).

This chapter also describes the story's setting and purpose. The setting is the creation, and the purpose is a relationship with God and humanity. The chapter reveals much about God and humanity through this creation and relationship. Furthermore, the closeness in this relationship is illustrated by the fact that God and humanity walked side by side (Genesis 3:8). It is clear that humanity has a freedom that the rest of creation does not have, and with that freedom comes additional responsibility. Also revealed in the chapter is that God, as the Creator and organizer of the world, plays a significant role in this relationship. God shared in the responsibility to maintain the media of creation but is not limited to it. In fact, God has stepped through the media, to save us from being lost on the other side, through incarnation. To describe this relationship, it is best to picture it linearly with humanity on one side, God on the other side, and creation in the middle. Thus, God creates and speaks to humanity through creation (Romans 8:19–20).

Furthermore throughout this chapter, much is revealed about God. God's identity as truth, holiness, and love becomes known and experienced as a reality in and apart from the creation (John 17:17; Genesis 18:25; 1 John 4:8). God is revealed as righteous, just, faithful, full of wisdom, holy, and stern (Isaiah 57:15; Exodus 15:11; Psalm 104:24; Romans 3:25–26; Joshua 23:14). In this paper I will refer to God in the singular number, even though there are three distinct divine entities. Although God is three, God is also one. God is revealed in three distinct entities known as the Father, the Son, and the Holy Spirit. God the Father illuminates the creative nature of God, God the Son illuminates the reconciling nature of God, and God the Holy Spirit illuminates the transformation and redemptive nature of God. Each part of this trinity or threeness of God is not limited to particular aspect of revelation. For example, all three aspects of God were present and active during creation, just as all three aspects of God were present and active in the atoning act of Christ (Genesis 1:26; Matthew 27:46). The three entities of God are each completely God and act to illuminate specific aspects of God, but they are wholly unified as one God.

The next chapter in the story is the fall of humanity. The first sin is described in Genesis 3 and represents the shortcomings of all of humanity. The sin was and always is the denial of God's original purpose, that humanity should be in constant relation to God and to each other. Sin is not being in proper relationship with humanity. There are countless examples of these kinds of sins throughout scripture. Crimes of adultery, fornication, and rage are a few that are addressed in the New Testament (Galatians 5:19–20). Sin is also an improper relationship with God. The denial of God's lordship and authority, the inappropriate care of creation, and the lack of service on behalf of God are a few examples. The Bible attests to the Israelites' struggle with trusting in God and their ability to worship only God. Therefore, the result of such sin, which is inevitable for fallen humanity, is separation from God and the intended relationship (Genesis 6:5; Romans 3:23; Romans 5:12). Furthermore, this sin is bondage that keeps humanity separated from God. The perfect relationship between God and humanity, which was created and intended by God, was broken and locked away by sin. The human situation was now in opposition to God's way and intentions.

At this point in the story, it seems as if evil is going to have the final word. It is a scene of despair, and the human situation looks as if it is out of reach from God. The plot thickens with a mood that is set in a suspenseful tone. The reality of this chapter speaks loud and clear in a culture that feels alienated from God, as my own context does. This human situation is our own situation prior to becoming and knowing the rest of the story. It is the situation that all people must move from in order to grasp the reality of God's revelation and presence in a particular context and a specific time. This chapter brings to light the destructive path of the human situation. However—and most fortunately—this chapter is not the final one.

The next chapter is the turning point of the entire story. Here a victory is won, and there is a new hope for relationship between God and humanity. This narrative apex is the central focus and pivotal point within Christianity. The apex is the coming of Jesus Christ. This event brings into clear focus God's intention to be in a relationship with humanity. The relationship is more than just a common understanding or acknowledgment, but rather intimate sharing and love between creation and Creator. This Christological event is known as the incarnation of God. The incarnation can be described in three distinct elements: humanity, divinity, and their unity. First is the humanity of Christ. It is quite clear that Christ was fully human (Matthew 4:1–2; Luke 2:52; John 4:5–6). The meaning behind this "flesh" goes far beyond a mere type of physical existence. Christ had not only a human body but human thoughts and emotions as well. He felt pain, discomfort, joy, and humor just like everybody else. It is this act of becoming human and sharing in the realities of life that make the humanity of Christ so significant.

The second element is the divinity of Christ. Because Christ was fully divine, he was fully God (Matthew 25:31–32; Mark 1:2–3; John 20:28; Acts 2:21; Ephesians 1:22–23). Jesus was neither a superhuman nor a heavenly figure; he was the embodiment of God. The Christ who had come to help us was God. Christ could perform miracles, heal people, set people free, and change lives. Additionally, Christ granted salvation, an act only God can do (Luke 23:39–43). Christ's focus was not on power but on forgiveness, love, and righteousness. This focus was truly divine and true to God's nature. The element is the unity of Christ. Christ was fully human and fully God in the same existence. Because Christ was both fully human and fully divine, his sacrifice of a perfect and sinless life was enough to take away the penalty of sin, and in fact, restore the intended relationship between God and humanity. The reality of the human situation could only have the possibility of reconciliation with God if this perfect and sinless sacrifice was made. In addition, it could be made available for all people only if it was from God. Only a sacrifice deemed worthy would have been able to set the world free from the bondage of sin and the human situation.

Beyond the personhood of Christ is the work of Christ as God's reconciling act. This reconciliation and restored life is known as atonement. In order to understand Christ's work here on earth, or his atonement, one must examine some important images. These images answer the *what*, the *why*, and the *how* of Christ's work. The *what* is answered by the image of genuine reconciliation. After the fall, there was nothing that was more sought after. Because the intimate relationship with God was lost as a result of the fall, Christ sought to make it possible once again. Throughout Christ's earthly ministry, he sought to show the world that he was the truth and the way to a restored relationship with God (John 5:36; John 14:6; Acts 10:36–38). The path of reconciliation with God was through the truth of Christ. This truth was a way to freedom through relationship with God. Throughout Christ's earthly ministry, he worked to liberate people from ideas, practices, and powers that were not truth. In fact, Christ came to set people free from the most oppressive power in contrast to truth: the power of sin. While Christ battled with these oppressive powers, even to his own death, he proved to be genuine truth, in whom there was none greater.

The question of *why* is answered by the image of Christ's love through his presence. Christ chose to become human in order to be the best manifestation of God's love for the creation. Because of the fall of humanity, the world was filled with people who felt unloved, unappreciated, and even despised. That God cared so much to come and be with humanity speaks a message of hope, encouragement, and empowerment. Death, disease, and hopelessness are understood and not ignored by God. The immortality and temporality of human life, along with its suffering, has been shared with the Creator. Through his presence, Christ is the bearer of good news, the good news of death not having the final say in life. Christ demonstrated this principle with his own life. The last question of *how* is answered by the image of sacrifice and obedience. In a world that is filled with sin and the results of unrighteousness, the need for forgiveness and new life is great. Because Christ sacrificed his life through crucifixion and death, the eternal penalty for sin can be erased (Isaiah 53:3–4; John 10:14–18; Galatians 3:13; Hebrews 9:14). Only a perfect sacrifice, fully human and fully divine, could have paid the price for the iniquities of humanity. Therefore, I believe reconciliation for humanity with God and itself was made possible.

The finality of Christ's work or atonement comes in his own resurrection. This resurrection is more than just a symbolic victory over sin and separation; it is a concrete verification to his earthly ministry with a new covenant (Luke 24:46; 1 Corinthians 15:4; Revelation 1:5). This new covenant is a unique relationship between God and humanity through the atonement of Christ (Matthew 26:28; Romans 11:27; Hebrews 7:22). Christ's role as mediator has once again brought together humanity and God (1

Timothy 2:5; Hebrews 8:6). The role of Christ as mediator is the part of the story that brings forgiveness and reunion into reality. It is the way we as individuals become part of the story. Christ's work of reconciliation between God and humanity becomes personal reconciliation for anyone who claims this story as his or her own. It is the start of a transforming relationship that moves one from isolation into communion with God and the community of God. It is a relationship with God through a new covenant.

Christ's work naturally leads to the next chapter in the story, salvation. This is the direction the story moves, in light of a new hope and new relationship with God, as it moves away from the human situation. This idea of salvation can be explained as a pardon from sin or as a justification (Psalm 32:1–2; Luke 18:14; Acts 18:39; Titus 3:5–7). It is a way in which those who claim the story can become free from blame. Furthermore, within salvation is the idea of sanctification as the process of becoming holy or worthy of a relationship with God (Philippians 3:12; Thessalonians 5:13; Hebrews 6:1; 1 John 1:8–9). Throughout the Bible, these ideas have been expressed in different contexts within the story. One such context is that Christ was a worthy sacrifice for all sin (1 John 2:1–2). This idea of salvation comes from the Old Testament understanding of the sacrificial laws. These laws describe sacramental requirements as a way of penitence or justification for sin. Through this context, Christ's death was a once-and-for-all event that eliminated the need for any other kind of burnt offering or sacrifice.

The next context contains the idea of being purified or cleansed (John 15:3; Hebrews 10:2). This idea is illustrated in scriptures by the need for lepers, or anyone who was unclean, to be cleansed by the priest and other religious authorities. There is an association between sin and being unclean. With this view, Christ's blood is the cleaning and purifying agent. The last view is the idea of being set free from prison or released from a sentence (Romans 6:17–18; Romans 8:1–2; Corinthians 7:22). This is best understood in light of some kind of judicial system. One is sentenced for a crime, and then Christ serves the sentence. Further, it is in this context that one can be set free from the captive nature of sin. The contextual nature of an understanding of salvation brings light to the way this story becomes our own. Though this work of Christ is done completely by divine initiative while calling for human acceptance and faith, we understand it in ways that relate to our own lives. This brings significant meaning and relevance into the way we claim the story and articulate it to others.

In this narrative, the following chapter helps bring meaning and understanding in light of the story's apex through the work of the Holy Spirit. This element of the story has been to work in each one of the preceding chapters with God and as God but comes into a new light in this chapter. The Holy Spirit resides in the life of one who has responded to God's offer of salvation. This Spirit's work is threefold. First, there is a sense of contradiction to nature and the human situation (Romans 8:26; 1 Corinthians 2:4, 11; Galatians 6:1). Assuming that nature is what comes naturally to somebody or simply an impulse to be what one is and to act accordingly, spiritually what is from God runs contrary to the nature the human situation and works according to God's standards for relationship. Second, this lifestyle is not lived solely by human will and strength, gut with strength from the spirit (Acts 16:6–7; Corinthians 1:21; Galatians 5:25; Philippians 11:19). Here the spirit exerts a gentleness that guides, directs, and empowers.

Third, the Spirit has the role of an intermediate between the "already" and the "not yet." The role of the Spirit here is to provide a glimpse of what lies ahead and to start preparing for the future (Romans 8:1–11; Romans 14:17; 2 Corinthians 5:5; Ephesians 1:12). It acts as a sort of beginning or first fruits, as the scripture describes. True spirituality is not yet present but will eventually come (Romans 8:22). Thus, the Spirit provides a taste of what is to come. God's ultimate work and presence in our lives has only begun through the presence of the Spirit and is yet to be completed (Philippians 1:6). I believe that life with the Spirit is both an outward manifestation and an inner empowerment. Outwardly, it is life that is lived apart from human nature and focused on things that are godly, while inwardly, it is driven and formed by the Holy Spirit.

The church is the next chapter in our story. The church is a universal body of believers who are in a growing relationship with God. The body is growing in faith as well, seeking to serve and telling the story of which it is a part. From this perspective, it is the communal aspect of the relational intention that God originally proposed for humanity. In the New Testament, the church is called the body of Christ (Romans 12:5; Corinthians 12:12; Ephesians 1:3–6). The story serves to bring humanity back into a relation with God, through Christ and the new covenant. There are four aspects of the church that are important to telling our story to the world in which we live. Each aspect, with its own distinctiveness, is an integral part of the other three. The first is the presence of the Spirit within the body of believers. This Spirit was given to the church at Pentecost as an act of empowerment and an official beginning of the work for the body of Christ (Acts 2). The significance of the spirit of the church can be summed up as empowerment, a source for direction, and connection to the "already" with the "not yet" on a communal level (1 John 3:2). Additionally, the Spirit has an adhesive property within the church by working in individual lives toward a unity of focus.

*Leitourgia* is the next aspect of the church. This is best thought of as the celebration within that causes an outside reaction. The special ordinances of baptism and the Lord's Supper are part of this celebration (Matthew 3:11; John 6:52). Through baptism, one makes a public confession of a new life through Christ. Baptism is the representation of the death of an old way of life in order to rise to a new life in Christ. The second ordinance is the Lord's Supper. Through this event the community remembers the life and death of Jesus. It is also a time when the community anticipates the fulfillment of the kingdom of God and renews commitment to Christ. The outside reaction of this celebration would be an overflowing of God's goodness and spirit. It is a way of illustrating the reality of the significance of the story. This aspect of the church causes spiritual growth in the body of believers (Ephesians 4:14–16; Colossians

2:19; Peter 2:1–3). The following aspect is known as *diakonis*. This is where the idea of service is added to the church. The church is to send its members out to care for the sick, homeless, and outcast in order to bring the story to life (Matthew 19:21; John 20:20; James 5:13–14). This aspect of service includes emotional, physical, and spiritual support. Furthermore, this service demonstrates the love and compassion involved in a relationship with God. The next aspect is *koinonia* or community. Here, the church body is called to gather under one purpose (Acts 2:44; Acts 5:1–10; Ephesians 6:23; 1 John 4:20–21). There should be commonality within the body of believers that is unparalleled. Paul describes this as a likeness of spirit and of mind (Philippians 1:27). This is not a requirement for identicalness but unity due to the common story of being in relation to God and the telling of it.

The purpose of the church is to tell the story of God's intention for relationship through the work and person of Jesus Christ. It is a story that is to be told universally and locally by the church. The local church is the community of God at the local level. It is a community where each member is in relationship with God and with each other. The local church can best answer the call to witness God's work and presence through evangelism, discipleship, ministry, fellowship, and worship. Evangelism is the story of good news spoken by believers and lived out in their lives. It is an intentional effort at telling the story through words, actions, and relationship-building. Discipleship is the growth that occurs in one's life through a relationship with Christ. This spiritual growth helps believers find their own calling and leadership potential. Discipleship leads to ministry, which is meeting the needs of others so that God's presence and working can be seen. Fellowship is the community of a body of believers that I have already described as koinonia. The last calling of the local church is worship. Worship is the gathering of the community to experience God in a meaningful and spiritually transforming way. It is the leitourgia of the local church.

The church as part of the story is moving and will eventually move to completion. This is the idea of consummation or the "not yet," which is the ultimate goal of the church in establishing the kingdom of God (Romans 8:19; Revelation 21:1–7). This future consummation was the goal of Christ's work in the kingdom of God. This new kingdom, which Christ started, will be the ultimate fulfillment of the relationship between God and humanity (Acts 1:3, 28:23; Romans 14:16; 1 Corinthians 4:20; Galatians 5:20). As humanity responds to the story and in the church, this kingdom is progressively being established. The "already" and the "not yet" come closer and closer together as the kingdom progresses toward culmination. At the center of this consummation is the story of Christ, for it is in response to his teachings and through faith in his saving work that humanity can be restored to a true relationship with God, the new covenant, and so enter the kingdom of God.

The reality of this coming kingdom is the eschatological theme found in scriptures. In review, our story reveals the creation, the fall of humanity, salvation through Christ, and the consummation. This thematic movement brings to the light the reality of God's intention to be in relationship with humanity. Furthermore, there is both a "realized" and a "future" aspect to this eschatology. Here, God's decisive eschatological act, through Christ, has already taken place. However, the consummation remains in the future. Thus, there is in this eschatology a sense of an "already" accomplished fulfillment and a "not yet" fulfillment still to come. The "already" sense was the beginning of the kingdom of God started by Christ, while the "not yet" sense is an important part of the story. The eschatological nature of our story is evident in the Bible from the call of Abraham and the promise of the land (Genesis 12:1–3). In the New Testament, it is evident through the revelation of the second coming of Christ. Although it cannot be known how or when, his coming is a sure reality (Matthew 24:36; 1 Peter 1:7, 13; Titus 2:13). Along with the second coming of Christ, there is the resurrection of God's people. This includes both the body and the soul. Resurrected bodies will somehow be physical and spiritual (John 11:25; Acts 4:2; 1 Corinthians 15:21–22, 42–44, 52). Just as there is a resurrection in our story, there will be judgment. The judgment will be unfortunate for some and glorious for others. The judge on this day will be Christ; this is appropriate because he is the one from whom salvation must be sought (Acts 17:31; Romans 2:16; 2 Peter 3:7; Jude 1:6). Eternity will be spent either with God or without God (Matthew 19:16; John 3:14–16, 17:2; Acts 13:46; Galatians 6:8).

The Christian lives this story between the "already" and the "not yet," between the resurrection of Christ and the future coming of Christ. This allows for a unique stage of Christian existence. It provides us with an opportunity to tell the story of Christ's saving work and God's desire for relationship through our thoughts, words, and actions. I believe that as the church, we are to tell about and live this story of God's intention for relationship through the work and person of Jesus Christ, as well as our own stories of God working in our lives. The telling of this story that lives and breathes through the tradition of the church, the revelation of God in scripture, and the context in which I live gives me substance, purpose, and hope in my own faith.

# Brahma Kumaris

Brahma Kumaris is a religion I had never heard of before starting this book. It was started in the 1930s by a Sindi businessman named Lekhraj Kripalani. He received a series of visions that inspired him to bring about transformation in the world. Religious practice is based on the Raja yoga form of meditation. This form of meditation allows for a person to reconnect with him or herself and reenergize the spirit. The four "guiding principles of Brahma Kumaris are: toward self is the principle of self-respect, toward God is the principle of cooperation, toward the material world is the principle of cooperation, and toward all people is the principle of benevolence."[4] The main headquarters of the organization is located at Mount Abu, Rajasthan, India. There are currently more than 825,000 students, with more than 8,500 centers in 110 countries and territories.

## Finding a Spokesperson

I was introduced to Brahma Kumaris by Seema Shah when she invited me to attend one of their services. After the service, Seema introduced me to Sister Lakshmi Akella. Sister Lakshmi is an extremely calm and warm individual who, after our initial meeting, asked me to drop by the Brahma Kumaris center, so we could speak more about my concept. After a few meetings, Sister Lakshmi agreed to participate in this project. She wanted to make it clear that she would write an essay and present this essay to her

---

[4] Brahma Kumaris World Spiritual Organization, copyright 1995–2007, www.brahmakumaris.org.

members before she would allow me to see it. Sister Lakshmi also wanted everyone to understand that the essay was her opinion and not the total meaning of Brahma Kumaris. The following is Sister Lakshmi Akella's essay, titled "Core Beliefs."

## By Sister Lakshmi Akella

## The Soul

The human is not a body but an eternal soul that lives in the body for the time being and is reincarnated from one body to another body. The soul is called "Atma" and is in the center of the forehead. This is where the "infinitesimal small point of spiritual light energy" of the body resides. Before the first soul enters the body, it comes from Paramdham, a place where all the souls rest before they have a body to enter. This is a place of infinite spiritual light. The soul is said to enter the body at about four months of pregnancy; this is what gives the mother's body its personality and light.

## God

We, the Brahma Kumaris, believe God to be a "soul" like everyone else and not having a physical body, as he does not take birth or rebirth, like human souls. However, the marked difference between human souls and God is that God is the perfect and constant embodiment of all virtues, powers, and values and that he is the father of all souls, irrespective of religions. It is believed that the Supreme Soul, God Shiva, is personally guiding and teaching Brahma Kumaris.

## Three Worlds

We believe that there are three different worlds:

1.  The physical universe: The physical world is where the souls are in the bodies to live their lives. This world consists of everything we can see and feel.
2.  Paramdham: This is the world of souls. This is where all the souls are to rest and experience peace and light before they enter their first-time body.
3.  The subtle regions: This is world of light, which can be reached through meditation. This world is full of light and peace, and the subtle regions are occupied by both Brahma Baba and the Supreme Soul, God Shiva. This is also the place where visions of this world and even the forthcoming golden age or *Satyuga* occur. Trance messengers of the Brahma Kumaris are able to travel to this region to seek advice and instructions on the running of the organization from Brahma Baba and God Shiva, collectively known as BapDada.

## Karma

We, the Brahma Kumaris, believe that karma plays an extensive role in deciding where and when we are born. The destiny of the soul's next body depends on how you act and behave in life. Through meditation, by transforming your thinking pattern and eventually your actions, you can absolve your sins and lead a better life in the next birth.

## The Cycle of Ages

Time is said to be a cycle that repeats every five thousand years. There are four ages, each of which lasts about 1,250 years. They are called the Golden Age, the Silver Age, the Copper Age, and the Iron Age. The Golden Age begins as a paradise where spiritual-minded souls who maintain the highest levels of purity, peace, and happiness live. This then leads to the Silver Age, where there is a slight and hardly noticeable decline in purity levels. After this age, the earth declines further into the Copper Age, where humanity experiences the duality of spirit and matter. Here, suffering is experienced for the first time; the search for God to ease suffering begins, and religions are created for the first time. Twelve hundred fifty years later, a totally impure Iron Age of suffering, injustice, and irreligious time begins, which personifies hell on earth. The fifth and current age, the Confluence Age, which lasts for about one hundred years, begins at the ending phase of the Iron Age. This is the age of disaster and mass destruction globally, at which time humanity makes a collective effort in regaining the peace, purity, and happiness they originally had.

With Raja yoga meditation, understanding of the self and God provides us with the following:

## Insight

The encounter, which is silent and very personal, often cannot be described. In some ways it shouldn't be described too much. In the silence there arises insight. Insight is the opening of the third eye, and spiritual blindness is taken away—in particular the blindness of being critical about things and people, of getting lost in weakness of others and caught up in trivial things. Insight is where you are able to see the positive reality of others, no matter what their appearance may be, no matter how negative they may appear to be. The insight of someone who has encountered God is to see through God's eyes, to be able to see others as one's brother or one's sister. It is this insight that starts to create a sense of unity and friendship and a sense of belonging to all.

## Inspiration

A personal encounter with God also gives us great inspiration. The impossible becomes possible. There's nothing we can't do. There is always that support, acceptance, and faithfulness from God in his relationship with us. He doesn't abandon, damage, or diminish you, but holds you. You are sacred to him. It is great inspiration when we feel this, not just knowing it intellectually but also feeling it.

From abstract to real, this is something for which we all have to make an effort. That comes from going into stillness, silence, and listening. After having this encounter, one's faith and courage are empowered. There are always tests, problems, difficulties, but one always has the strength to overcome them, because one is now able to look and see with another "eye." One sees with an invisible eye, hears with another ear, an invisible ear. You do not have to see everything tangible in front of you. You don't have to see the solution, because you know it's there and will come at the right time. The person who has a genuine encounter and ongoing experience develops a lot of kindness, generosity, tolerance, and especially nonviolence. That person never thinks he or she is better, superior, or inferior to another. There is a feeling of equality with others—that others are as good as me, that whatever good I have in my own self others have also.

When we have that genuine encounter with God, the vision of universality is restored, and there is an attention to personal change and giving. There is never an inflated sense of superiority. However, many forget to protect their genuine encounter with God with humility and self-respect. Instead they start to say, "I saw this vision, I saw this light, and I got this message." So what did I do with the message, with the light? Did I grow? Growth is measured by the respect I have for others and the nonviolent attitude toward all things. I accept any differences as something divine and enhancing for the world; I realize such differences do not limit but enrich.

When we have an encounter with God, we experience God's fatherhood, God's motherhood, and above all God's sweet friendship. Yes, the ancient Egyptians were very right: God the Father, the Mother, is the Lord of sweetness, and it is that sweetness that takes the bitterness of the past and enables us to experience the power of forgiveness, to let go of things, not hold any grudges. When there is that forgiveness for your own self, then you can start to realize who you can really be.

This love-filled transformation makes a human being spiritual. A true relationship transforms and frees you; it does not bind and limit. When we encounter God as he truly is, our consciousness ascends to a level of universality and compassion where there are no barriers of resentment, accusation, or fear.

To be able to keep your courage, faith, and principles, even in times of opposition, and to keep a kind eye on those who oppose you — this is spiritual! This is the ability to have mercy and compassion toward those who criticize and oppose you. It's not just a question of being stable and strong but having a kind eye for everyone. For that we require the sustenance of a personal relationship with God, or else we can't have compassion. If you don't feel that relationship, you can be kind once or twice to people who are negative toward you, but to stay compassionate requires a very positive, continuous flow of strength within yourself. This is why meditation is important, not just for self but also for others. It's in meditation that you get close to God and experience the power he is constantly offering you. This closeness to God is called bliss. Bliss is an experience that is internal, beyond touch, sight, or anything physical, and no one can ever take that away from you. You carry it within yourself.

# Church of Christ

The Church of Christ is a breakout group from the Church of Latter-Day Saints (Mormon). "The church accepts the King James Version of the Bible and the Book of Mormon as its standard."[5] The church does not accept all of the revelations as stated by Joseph Smith, due partly to the changes that were made to the early revelations. The "Church of Christ prefers to use The Book of Commandment to Doctrine and Covenants which includes change."[6] The church does not accept plurality of gods, baptism for the dead, or plural marriage.

## Finding a Spokesperson .

I called Reverend Woods's church a few times before we met. I was always greeted by an extremely nice secretary, who later set up an appointment for me with Reverend Woods. When I first met with Reverend Woods, I told him how nice his secretary sounds on the phone, and he told me I was talking to his wife. Reverend Woods is a kind and pleasant individual who makes you feel at ease in his presence. He is very active in his community and has offered the church in which he officiates to be used for many community events. When asked if he would participate in my project, he agreed immediately. The following is Reverend Roger Woods's essay, titled "What Is My View of God?"

---

[5] Frank S. Mead and Samuel S. Hill, *Handbook of Denominations in the United States 11th Edition*, revised by Craig D. Atwood (Nashville: Abington Press, 2001), 198.

[6] Ibid.

## By Reverend Roger B. Woods

This is one of the most important questions you can ask and answer; how you answer it frames your worldview and therefore how you interact with this world. An atheist denies the existence of any morally authoritative force outside the material world; therefore, he interacts with the world based primarily on self-interest. A traditional animistic religionist views God as a force that can be manipulated but is also to be feared. Therefore, he interacts with the world in a way that avoids the wrath of the spirits but also tries to manipulate them to favorably help him. If you view God as a deist, you move him to the margins of life and for all practical purposes only expect help from him in emergencies—if then. He becomes the God of the gaps at best and of little use in this life. Contrastingly, if the deity is a personal God, he will play a role in every aspect of my life, and I will base my decisions with the understanding that he is present as I make them.

I believe God is personal, living, and active. He is all-knowing, all-powerful, and ever-present. How I came to this belief is the product of many influences and factors. These start with foundational influences, such as the family and faith community in which I was raised and continue with developmental influences, such as mentors, professors, authors, finally confirmed through personal experiential factors—how I see others experience God and how I have felt his presence in my life.

## Foundations

I was born into a God-fearing Christian family who made participation in church a first priority. My parents came to their faith in God through Jesus Christ in different ways. My father was raised in a family who seldom went to church. His mother was a Methodist, and his father was, for all practical purposes, a pantheist. My dad came to faith after serving in two wars and having begun a family. My mother's family was, by way of contrast, highly involved with their church, and it is within this faith tradition that I was raised. Indeed my mother's funeral service was held in the very church and in front of the pool in which she was baptized as a young teen.

In my family, church participation was never optional, yet we were invited into and made a part of a loving fellowship of believers who believe that they are the body of Christ on earth. As a part of that body, they held the conviction that what they do really matters here on earth and in God's eternal reality. The Churches of Christ are part of a religious movement often called the Restoration Movement. It sought and continues to seek to restore Christianity to its biblical foundation and away from the creedal and traditional stances of denominations. They seek to be "just Christians" as they study the scriptures to discover who God is, how we come to know him, and how we should serve him.

One of the areas that made God real to me was in the corporate worship. The fellowship of the Churches of Christ in which I was raised does not use instrumental accompaniment with singing. We practiced a cappella and congregational singing—we sang a lot, and I loved it! Singing about "Marching to Zion" and of a "New Song" did more to form my faith than many of the classes I attended in college. If heaven were better than this, then it was a place I wanted to be! Though not perfect, my childhood faith developed through both my spiritual and blood families leading me to accept God and see him as an active part of my life.

How he was a part of my life became more defined as I matured, but my childhood demonstrated that God was an active force on earth and that his people in the church were my family—wherever I might live. This last point was very important, for I was raised in a navy family. When I was born, my dad was seventeen years into a thirty-year career. I was born in Connecticut, and before I left home, I had lived in Illinois, Iowa, Hawaii, California, Virginia, and New Jersey. Besides my own family, the church was the only other constant I had—yes, different people but all with shared core beliefs and practices—not perfect but sacred. It was within this larger family that I came to having faith in Jesus as my Savior and was baptized into him in 1970 on my eleventh birthday. I had come to believe that God was real and that he had work for all to do, important work that I could share in.

## Development

I grew up, and so did my faith and my understanding. God, the Holy Spirit, and Jesus became real to me and not just some good lines from some of my favorite hymns. This development came in part from the formal educational process in the church. (Looking back, I had good teachers who taught me about God through their lives and understanding of scripture.) Later it was deepened through my formal education at religious colleges, universities, and seminaries. But central to this maturing understanding of God was the centrality of scripture when it comes to knowing him.

God reveals himself in many ways, but scripture (Old and New Testament) is the controlling document. Paul wrote to Timothy that "All Scripture is God-breathed (inspired) and is useful for teaching, rebuking, correcting and training in righteousness" (2 Timothy 3:16 NIV). Speculation upon the nature of God is just that, if it has no basis in the Bible. We learn from scripture that God has been about the business of revealing himself from the beginning. The apostle Paul even notes that the Lord uses his creation as a witness to his existence (Acts 17). The writer of the New Testament letter to the Hebrews notes that "In the past God spoke to our forefathers through the prophets at many times and in various ways, but in these last days he has spoken to us by his Son, whom he appointed heir of all things, and through whom he made the universe" (Hebrews 1:1–2 NIV). Along with all other Christians, I believe Jesus Christ is the ultimate and authoritative revelation of God. Indeed he is the "exact representation of the Father" (Hebrews 1:3 NIV).

I would offer this brief outline of my formal understanding of God.

He is eternal and exists in eternal community of Father, Son, and Holy Spirit. In this, Churches of Christ believe in the standard

Trinitarian formulations inasmuch as they are supported by the clear teaching of scripture.

He created the universe through his Son Jesus Christ (John 1).

He created man with free will to share in his holy community, but man rejected God and sought to make his own way (Genesis 1–3).

He is all-powerful and all-knowing. But he is not all-controlling. He established the universe and its laws but intercedes when necessary to further his mission of reconciliation.

God has, since the Fall, been seeking to redeem this lost relationship. His efforts are plainly seen in the narrative of the Old Testament as he patiently led Israel to understand and accept him as their Lord.

In his passion for redeeming fallen humankind, he knew he would need to take on our form for us to understand him. He did this in Jesus of Nazareth who was God's chosen one (anointed one / Messiah / Christ).

His redemptive effort for all humankind was completed in Jesus's suffering, death, and resurrection and is available to all those who through faith accept and submit to him as Lord.

He gave the risen Jesus all power and authority, and this Lord then sent the Holy Spirit to live within each believer and in the church.

In and through Christ, he restored the relationship with God lost in the garden of Eden as he dwells within us through his Holy Spirit.

He will come again to judge the living and the dead according to his word and their deeds in this life.

## Experiential

As I write this final section, my church is in the midst of forty days of spiritual meditation and prayer. Our theme is from Jeremiah 9, where God reveals his message for Israel to Jeremiah at the potter's house. There the potter molds the clay into the type of vessel he sees as useful. Israel is the clay — I am the clay — and God is the potter. He uses many tools to form and shape me. Chief of these is my life experience. Learning the lessons he wishes is up to us, but if we are trusting and observant, we can see how our Lord has molded us into useful items of service. Through victory and disappointment, elation and dejection, his hand is upon us — not causing our pain, though he has the right, but rather walking with us through it all, even the valley of the shadow of death.

I have experienced God's voice in the words of his servants and his holy scripture. I have felt his presence upon the mountaintops of emotional joy and in the valley of dejection and despair. Doors that were closed were opened; lives that were too far gone were turned around. Hope that was absent was found. As the apostle Paul wrote, I have come to be content in all circumstances because I believe my God is real, aware, and concerned for me and for all who look to him in faith. Do I have doubt? Yes, yet in the face of the cloud of witnesses surrounding me, I confess with the saints of all ages that our God lives and has considered my condition and saved me through his Son and sustains me by his Spirit.

This is my view of God upon which I stake my life now and forevermore.

# Conservative Judaism

Conservative Judaism was brought to America in 1913 by Solomon Schechter. The fundamentals of the religion are that Judaism should adapt to the surroundings and still follow the Torah (the first five books of the Bible: Genesis, Exodus, Leviticus, Numbers, and Deuteronomy) and *Halakah*, which is the set of rules and practices for everyday life that are based on Jewish law. Education is important in Conservative Judaism, and in most synagogues all aspects of Jewish life are taught. Each congregation is independent and has the right to accept or reject the recommendations set by the National Committee on Jewish Law and Standards.

## Finding a Spokesperson

I called the synagogue where Rabbi Pachter officiates, and he was gracious enough to set up time to meet with me in his office. Rabbi Pachter was extremely kind and sincere in our discussion. When I asked for his participation in helping to put this book together, he turned me down. A few hours later, I received a call from Rabbi Pachter, and he stated that he had a sermon for me that may answer the question of "who is God?" The sermon was given on the second day of Rosh Hashanah (a high holy day that celebrates the Jewish New Year). The following is the sermon.

## By Rabbi Elliot Pachter

[I have attempted to explain, in simple terms, what many of the Hebrew words mean.]

A good piece of advice from the business world can help us all. It guides me in choosing what to teach during a sermon. The advice is: there are two rules for succeeding in business. The first is: never tell them everything you know.

Now a question if God wore *tefillin* [A set of small black boxes with black straps attached to them. One box is worn on the head and the other on the arm. The boxes are biblical in origin. Inside the boxes are handwritten scrolls of parchment that are inscribed with verses from the Torah. The tefillin are worn for morning prayers during the week by Conservative and Orthodox Jewish males.], what would be written on the parchment inside? Our tefillin contains, among other words, the *Shema* [affirmation], reminding us that God is one. But God doesn't need a reminder of that.

By now, thinking I'm crazy, you're probably wondering why I even suggested that God would wear tefillin. But this is exactly what is suggested in rabbinic literature. First, look at the High Holy Day Supplement on page 19. You will need to trust my translation, because the translation on pages 21–22 does not accurately reflect this Hebrew phrase:

*Kesher tefillin her'a l'antov.*

He showed the humble one the knot of his tefillin.

The humble one is Moses, and this line refers to the time when Moses requested to see God's face, and God said *all you can see is my back*. With God facing away from him, Moses saw not only God's back but also the knot of tefillin on the back of God's head.

This is, anyway, the understanding of Rabbi Yehudah HaChasid of Regensburg (from the early thirteenth century), the author of "Shir Hakavod" ("Song of Glory"). But at least seven centuries earlier, the Babylonian Talmud (Berakhot 6a) [The Talmud contains the writings of Jewish tradition.] expresses the same idea, including answering my opening question.

Rabbi Nahman bar Isaac said to Rabbi Hiyya bar Abin: *What is written in the tefillin of the Lord of the Universe?* He replied to him: *Who can be compared to your people Israel, a unique nation upon the earth* (1 Chronicles 17:21)? For the benefit of those who are familiar with the Amidah for Shabbat Minchah [type of prayer for Sabbath afternoon], written in the tefillin of God is:

*Umee k'amkha Yisrael goy echad ba'aretz*
(Who is like your people Israel, a nation one in the earth?)

Our tefillin say: God is *echad* (one).
God's tefillin say: Israel is echad (one).

Again, like yesterday, I take you back to *birkhot hashachar*, the early-morning blessing; to another *berakhah* [blessing] whose wording has changed in most Conservative *siddurim* [prayer books]. The traditional liturgy says, *Barukh she'lo asani ishah*—intended for a man to declare joy at having the maximum number of *mitzvoth* [good deeds done from religious duty] to observe. Instead men and women say *barukh she'asani b'tzalmo*—I am grateful to be made in God's image.

And we also return to the three Bs (blessings), for this is our daily affirmation of belief. The God in whom I believe—I wear tefillin to remember him; he wears tefillin to remember me. Quite an image!

If only it were so easy to believe. We are halted in our spiritual tracks, though, because most of us can't truly sense that image in our minds, in our souls. For many, God is what we read about in the Torah, in the *Machzor* [prayer book for High Holidays] today, and in the *siddur* [prayer book] throughout the year. But face it, it's hard to believe.

If that is how you feel, I am sympathetic, but I'm not going to let you off the hook so easy. As I said yesterday, being a Jew, being *yisrael*, is a struggle. Finding God takes effort.

Some get to feel the closeness of God's presence. In 1 Kings 18, the prophet Elijah gathers the Israelites, builds an altar, pours water over the sacrificial bull three times, and prays, "Answer me O Lord, answer me, that this people may know that You, O Lord, are God." Fire descends from heaven and consumes everything, whereupon the people fling themselves on their faces and cry out, "The Lord alone is God! The Lord alone is God!"

Jewish Theological Seminary professor Neil Gillman, in his book, *Traces of God*, comments that he wishes he were granted what Elijah was—irrefutable proof of God's existence. But he knows that Elijah's story is an exception. Nonetheless, Dr. Gillman helps the rest of us, yisrael, in a successful struggle to discover the God who is sometimes/often hard to recognize.

Knock, knock. (Who's there?) Nobody (Nobody who?) Exactly. There's something out there; sometimes it's a voice that can't be heard.

Regarding this Elijah story, Jewish philosopher Emil Fackenheim asks, what would Elijah have done if God had not answered his call? Fackenheim, answering his own question says with certainty, one thing is clear: Elijah would have continued to work for God, even in the face of God's silence.

This comment reminds us of the recent stories of Mother Teresa, whose posthumously discovered letters describe a decades-long crisis of faith, during which time she did not truly feel God's presence. But what did she do? She continued to attend to the neediest of Calcutta. Even if you don't feel God's presence, it is still our duty to do God's work.

A billboard contains a quotation from God, saying: Do you think I sit around and wonder if you exist?

Deuteronomy 4:3, in reminding us how to recognize God's presence in our lives and in the world, says simply, "Your eyes have seen what the Lord did." If you can't see God, surely you can see the results of God's work.

We look around at the world, the wonders of nature, continuing discovery in the science lab, the advancement of medicine, the miracles of our own bodies and those of our children, and how can we not see the hand of God at work?

Rabbi Ephraim Buchwald, founding director of the National Jewish Outreach Program, in helping people to learn to believe in God, uses a similar approach. Just look at history. Look at how many times the Jewish people were enslaved, persecuted, murdered, exiled. Time after time, what looked like utter destruction instead led to a new beginning. Annihilation was averted, not once, not twice, but over and over again throughout the centuries. How can this be explained? Rabbi Buchwald gives us two choices — God is looking out for us, or this has been a series of coincidences; hundreds of times in a row, coincidentally, the Jews have had the talent or the luck to escape extinction. Rabbi Buchwald says, if we truly look at our history, how can you not believe in God? Frankly it takes more effort to believe in coincidence.

How many times in our lives is God present, and we just fail to notice? Many of you know the story of the man who lives alone on an island. He receives a letter from the mainland — "Get off the island. A violent storm is approaching." The man says to himself, *If God wanted me to leave the island, then God will tell me. Otherwise I am staying right here.*

The rain begins to pour, the water level is rising. A boat appears, and a voice calls from the boat, "Get off the island, climb aboard. There's going to be a flood." The man replies, "If God wants me to get off the island, God will tell me."

The water is up to the man's neck. A helicopter appears overhead. A rope ladder is lowered. A voice cries out, "Climb up the ladder. Come aboard the helicopter. It's your last chance!" The man replies, "Only God can tell me when it's time to leave."

The man drowns. He dies and comes face to face with God. The man begins to cry out, "Why didn't you save me from drowning?"

God replies, "I sent you a letter, I sent you a boat, I sent you a helicopter. What more could I have done?"

Therefore, it is in wisdom that our rabbis help us see God's hand when others only see human success. So on Chanukah [Festival of Lights], and also Yom HaAtzmaut [Israeli Independence Day], we raise to say *Hallel* [Psalm 113–118 that incorporate gratitude for God's past acts of salvation and confidence in God's future redemption of Israel]. Human-fought victories, to bring freedom and independence to the Jews of Israel, are indeed marked by gratitude to God.

On a more personal level, my sudden incapacity three months ago helped open my eyes to the presence of God. I am humble before you because many of you have already learned these lessons under much more challenging circumstances than I, but nonetheless, let me tell you about my own self-discovery during times of pain, adjusting to the temporary loss of mobility, and ultimately finding my way back to healing.

A few weeks ago at physical therapy, I watched a young girl, a high school student, who must have had knee surgery, being asked by the therapist to walk for the first time since her surgery, with only one crutch instead of two. I could see on the young woman's face the look of despair and hopelessness as she desperately tried to get a reluctant leg to move.

My own experience came back to me. It wasn't so long ago that I was told, "Try walking," and I truly thought it was a crazy idea. I thought I couldn't do it.

Shortly after my surgery, I spoke with a young man I know who had the same injury as me—ruptured Achilles tendon—three months prior to mine. He told me he was about to resume jogging. I remember thinking how unbelievable that sounded.

Here I am myself, three months to the day after surgery, not quite ready to jog, but far beyond where I thought I would be at this time. God exists in pain, in the masterful technique of the doctor who knows how to do the surgery. In God's wisdom, our bodies are created in a way that so often, we miraculously recover from injury and surgery.

I found God in the patience I needed to endure and in the hope that it would get better.

But for those who don't get better, who live with pain and illness, God also is their source of inner strength, to put up the best fight they have, not to be defeated.

I read a painful story recently of a baby born with a rare form of blindness. He will never see. His parents' reaction began with confusion and despair, but ultimately, they returned to loving their child, appreciating how beautiful he is, and most importantly, learning to patiently allow their son to learn how to cope with blindness at his own pace. The child finds his way around the house and the world and is a constant source of joy and reminder of God's blessing.

One more way we find the elusive God is found in a strange story concerning Abraham. Genesis 18 begins, "Then the Lord appeared to Abraham." But in the next verse, Abraham sees only men, not God. He welcomes the strangers into his home to be his guests. We might only see people, but when we reach out to help, we are recognizing the presence of God.

Yes, we can find God in nature, in history, in the faces of those we love, in our inner strength that we never realize we had. But remember the image of God wearing tefillin. It is not only we who seek God; God also seeks us.

A burglar, attempting to rob a home, hears a voice: *God is watching you. God is watching you.* The burglar then realizes that the voice is that of a parrot. He asks the parrot, "What is your name?" The parrot replies, "Saint Peter." The burglar then asks, "What kind of a person would name a parrot Saint Peter?" The parrot replies, "The same person who names his Rottweiler God!"

God, donned in tefillin, seeks out the people of Israel, unique among the nations. To live up to God's high expectations means to be a people who believe in God's presence, even when it is a challenge to do so, recognizing God's role behind all our triumphs, God's comforting hand during our hour of despair, and God's holy image deep within ourselves and within the spirit of each of our fellow human beings.

# *Episcopalian*

The Protestant Episcopal Church has been called the Episcopal Church in the United States since 1967. The religion allows for variations in each church for independent thinking, individuality, and religious liberty. Clergy of the Episcopal Church believe that the Old and New Testaments are the words of God and that these testaments contain everything needed for salvation. The two major tenets of the church are the Apostles' Creed and the Nicene Creed. The church also follows articles of the Church of England with certain modifications. "Adherence to them as a creed is not required."[7] All Episcopal churches follow two sacraments: baptism and the Eucharist (communion.) In 1976, the church allowed women into the priesthood.

## Finding a Spokesperson

I meet Reverend Chris Yaw at the church in which he officiates. Reverend Yaw is an Emmy Award–winning journalist and author of several books. He did not have the time to help me on this project but gave me Reverend Henry Idema's phone number. I talked with Reverend Idema, and he offered to help on this book. Reverend Idema is a journalist whose articles have been published in various newspapers. After reading a number of Reverend Idema's articles, I was amazed at how much I agreed in principle with many of his

---

[7] Frank S. Mead and Samuel S. Hill, *Handbook of Denominations in the United States 11th Edition*, revised by Craig D. Atwood (Nashville: Abington Press, 2001), 133.

ideas. The following is Reverend Henry Idema's essay, titled "How Do We Know the Divine?"

## By Reverend Henry Idema

The theologian Paul Tillich argued at the conclusion of his important book, *The Courage to Be*, that God transcends the God of traditional theism. In other words, the monotheistic religions, Judaism, Christianity, and Islam, all point to a divine being and claim to reveal God, but their statements about God are all symbolic and fall short of fully describing the divine, which is unknowable.

It is my view that all the world religions, including Native American religions, point to a creative divine power that truly exists, but none of these religions adequately captures the true nature of the divine as God actually is.

From my Christian perspective, the Gospel of John says it best: "No one has ever seen God; the only Son, who is in the bosom of the Father, he has made him known" (1:18).

This is the idea of revelation. God is unknowable in and of himself, but God reveals himself in people, such as Jesus, in events, such as the Exodus, and in the words of the prophets, such as Jeremiah.

I know that my Christian faith can be partly explained by my upbringing in a Christian family in a Christian church in a Christian community. All religions are culture bound in terms of their origins and our own participation. Today, however, through education and the Internet, we are exposed to other religions in a way that was not as possible in, for example, a remote medieval town in France. Christians might know Jews in such a town and maybe even Muslims. But now our opportunities to know religions other than our own are vast. I have studied in graduate school the world religions, and I am persuaded that my religion works best for me. I can say without arguing that other religions are false. They just do not appeal to me as much as Christianity, and within Christianity, my Episcopal church. I also know the culture bond of my claims.

We live in a pick-and-choose age, in terms of not only religions but also denominations. If a religion meets your needs—need for love and community, for example—that religion will have great appeal. If your religion does not meet your needs, chances are you will neglect it and be bored by it, including the God it proclaims.

We live in an era where one can easily investigate the religions of the world and their claims about God. Language barriers make it hard to understand Islam, for example, or even the New Testament. Jesus spoke in Aramaic, and the New Testament was written in Greek, and in America, most read the Bible in English. Even with that limitation, the student of religion can reach conclusions about any religion's claims about God. Such claims will appeal to you or they won't. The most important point is realizing that all claims about God are bound by culture and history and language and symbolism. Thus these claims are only approximate truths.

God—for me the God of the history of the Bible—is truly unknowable. However, God has left footprints for us to follow in all the great religions. The path you choose to follow will be the path that for you leads to truth and best meets your needs.

Jesus, through his teachings about love and service to the poor and needy, is for me the most persuasive revelation of the nature of God, here God as love. If you value love above all else, then the God Jesus taught about and proclaimed will have great appeal to the heart as well as the mind. Jesus taught that such a God makes claims on us and commands us to love and serve. The God of Jesus demands for us mercy, compassion, love, and service, especially for the most needy. We know this God through action even more than through study and worship.

Paul Tillich said faith is our ultimate concern, or as Jesus put it, where the heart is, there your treasure will be. There are many competing "gods" in our culture—money and power, for instance.

Jesus saw that in his own culture. His God makes a claim on us in terms of discipleship over and above all the competing claims in a culture. Which God we choose to follow and believe in will, as Jesus taught, be known by our fruits.

To sum up, God is ultimately unknowable. As Paul says in 1 Corinthians 13:12, "For now we see in a mirror dimly, but face to face." In other words, our knowledge of God is limited, but there will come a time when we will know the truth fully. As Paul concludes in the same chapter, "Now I know in part; then I shall understand fully, even as I have been fully understood." And before that day comes, we will hold on to these truths: "Faith, hope, and love. Abide, these three; but the greatest of these is love" (13:12–13).

Love is the closest we come to knowing God this side of paradise.

# Hare Krishna

Hare Krishna, also called the International Society of Krishna Consciousness, is a form of Hinduism "founded in the United States in 1965 by A. C. Bhaktivedanta."[8] Bhaktivedanta is also known as Swami Prabhupada (1896–1977). Hare Krishna is based on the Krishna consciousness movement that began in the sixteenth century, in which believers used repetitive chanting in pursuit of mystical devotion. "The teachings of the Hare Krishna movement are derived from ancient Hindu scriptures, especially the Srinad-Bhagvatum and Bhagavad-Gita. Adherents believe that Krishna (an avatar of Vishnu) is the Supreme Lord and that humans are eternal spiritual beings in a cycle of reincarnation."[9] This cycle is determined by, "the law of consequences of past actions."[10] Karma can be broken by either extreme forms of yoga or by reciting the holy names Krishna and Rama. Believers spend several hours a day reciting the Hare Krishna mantra: "Hare Krishna, Hare Krishna; Krishna, Krishna, Hare, Hare; Hare Rama, Hare Rama; Rama Rama, Hare Hare." Hare Krishna devotees are vegetarians, reject the use of alcohol and drugs, and allow sex for procreation within marriage. Male adherents have a sikha, a small tuft of hair, on their shaved heads, and both males and females put clay on their foreheads in the morning to remind themselves that their bodies are temples of Krishna.

---

[8] John Gordon Melton, *Encyclopedia Britannica*, "Hare Krishna Religious Sect," www.britannica.com/topic/Hare-Krishna.

[9] Ibid.

[10] Ibid.

## Finding a Spokesperson

I met Ekantadas at the Hara Krishna temple in Detroit, where he is a priest. We had a vegetarian lunch, and I told him about the book I was compiling. Ekantadas listened intently and stated that he thought the book would be beneficial for people, since they will be able to see how different and yet simultaneously alike we all are. He also offered his assistance to work on this project. In his kindness, Ekantadas gave me the Bhagavad-Gita (a Hindu devotional work written in poetic form) to help me learn and understand more about Hare Krishna. The following is Ekantada's essay, "Who Is Krishna?"

## By Ekantadas

All of the following descriptions of Krishna are based on the teachings of the founder of the International Society for Krishna Consciousness, His Divine Grace, Srila A. C. Bhaktivedanta, Swami Prabhupad.

It is he who says, in the Bhagavad-Gita chapter 7, verse 8: "O Son of Kunti, I am the taste of water, the light of the sun and the moon, the syllable om [sic] in the Vedic mantras; I am the sound in either and_ability_in man." Who gives us the ability to see, hear, reason, choose, and make decisions. Therefore, he is giving us the privilege of being able to have the life, his energy is. We are God's energy. Because more important than the eyes' *ability*_to "see God" is the ears'_*ability*_to hear, and the mind's *ability* to receive, interpret, and send a message of acceptance or rejection to the brain. We think we choose to accept or reject, but God claims to be the one who is actually giving you the ability to make any decision you make!

God has created laws governing the forces of material nature (what drives our senses into action) that actually move us to make the decisions we say we make by choice. We have the free will to choose to the extent that we are actually "free" from the forces of nature that prompt us to make the decisions we make. Otherwise we are controlled by the external, material energy of God. When the senses of our bodies are the underlying motive for the decisions we make, based on what will make us more comfortable here, we should know we are being controlled by the senses of the body. This is one reason Krishna comes to this planet: to free us from the modes of nature which compel (force) us to action.

Bhagavad-Gita chapter 4, verse 8 says, "To deliver the pious and to annihilate the miscreants, as well as to reestablish the principles of religion, I Myself appear, millennium after millennium." In this way, we can understand how much God cares for humankind. He comes here personally to make a way for us to return to him.

So much has been said about God's creation of "heaven and hell," I feel it necessary to clarify for you our understanding of the heavens and hells of creation. We see the dwellings created for the pious in the heavenly realms as a place of reward for pious activities done in the middle planetary systems. When the benefits of the pious acts are used up, however, the souls have to return to the middle or lower planetary systems, again taking part in their karma. Hells are created for punishments of the living entities that deny the existence of God and insist on leading corrupt lives, even though the Supreme has made a way for them to become free. Their punishments are awarded only according to the severity of the activities they engaged in, nothing more, nothing less (not eternal fire). When the punishments are lived out, the residents of the hellish planets also return (according to their karma) to the middle planets to continue in the cycle of birth, death, and old age. It is only by direct contact with one who is freed from that cycle (*samsara*) or with one who knows one who is actually freed from the clutches of illusion that one can himself become free. The spiritual world (the kingdom of God) is far removed from this universe, which is but one small universe among (countless) millions of universes.

As for the mercy of God, it needs to be known that although in previous ages when a person committed a sinful act or even thought to do evil, he or she would get an immediate reaction.

In this age (called Kali Yuga), God is so kind that if you think to do evil in your mind but you do not act on it, God does not hold you accountable, but if you think to do good, he gives you credit as though you had performed the deed. That's mercy! I can only pray and hope to be able to describe God in a way that is pleasing to him. Rather than describe what he looks like, I realize it would be better to know his nature and the nature of his appearance and activities. What people look like tells us a lot about them, but what they do, what they say, and what they believe tell us more. Generally people like to meditate (when they pray) on the God they see from within (according to their faith), and God knows every faith and every soul.

Krishna seems to suggest it is very important to know the nature of his appearance and activities by making the following statement in the Bhagavad-Gita chapter 4, verse 9: "One who knows the transcendental nature of My appearance and activities does not, upon leaving the body, take his birth again in this material world, but attains My eternal abode, O Arjuna."

It certainly would be great if everyone who read this essay got enough information from this writing to be able to understand "the transcendental Nature of My appearance and activities," as Krishna gives a promise, which says he has the power to do something only God could do! In one sentence, he gives humankind (if what he says is true) an easy way out of this bondage of birth, death, old age, and disease, promising us an "abode" with him. With this in mind, I am going to delve into the nature of Krishna's appearance, as taken from the *Krishna Book*.

The founder of the International Society for Krishna Consciousness, His Divine Grace, Srila A. C. Bhaktivedanta, Swami Prabhupad, has so kindly given to the world this *Krishna Book*. Scholars will find the works of A. C. Bhaktivedanta Swami both pertinent and educational. Yet, this *Krishna Book* can be read to children of all ages; this *Krishna Book* is given in story form, unlike the sacred verses used in the other texts of our reference library.

11. Lord Siva: He is a "Guna Avatar" of the Supreme Lord, controlling the modes of ignorance. There are three gunas and three guna avatars controlling goodness, Visnu, passion, Brahma, and ignorance, Siva.

12. The Manus and the prajapatis are creators who can produce any form of life from their own body without another gender's aid. Hopefully by your reading this presentation and realizing the import of Krishna's statements, we can experience, together the unfolding of Krishna's pastimes. By revealing the activities of Krishna, we reveal Krishna. As stated in the Bhagavad-Gita, the Lord says that his appearance, births, and activities are all transcendental, and one who understands them factually becomes immediately eligible to be transferred to the spiritual world. The material body according to his past deeds. Lord's appearance or birth is not like that of an ordinary man who is forced to accept.

The Lord's appearance is explained in the second chapter of the *Krishna Book* as follows:

He appears out of His own sweet pleasure. When the time was mature for the appearance of the Lord, the constellations became very auspicious. The astrological influence of the star known as Rohini[1] was also predominant because this star is considered to be very auspicious. Rohini is under the direct supervision of Brahma.[2] According to the astrological conclusion, besides the proper situation of the stars, there are auspicious and inauspicious moments due to the different situations of the different planetary systems. At the time of Krishna's birth, the planetary systems were automatically adjusted so that everything became auspicious. At that time, in all directions, east, west, south, north, everywhere, there was an atmosphere of peace and prosperity. There were auspicious stars visible in the sky, and on the surface in all towns and villages or pasturing grounds and within the minds of everyone there were signs of good fortune. The rivers were flowing full of waters, and lakes were beautifully decorated with lotus flowers. The forests were full with beautiful birds and peacocks. All the birds within the forests began to sing with sweet voices, and the peacocks began to dance along with their consorts. The wind blew very pleasantly, carrying the aroma of different flowers, and the sensation of bodily touch was very pleasing. At home, the *brahmanas*,[3] who were accustomed to offer sacrifices in the fire, found their homes very pleasant for offerings. Due to disturbances created by the demoniac kings, the sacrificial fire altar had been almost stopped in the houses of *Brahmans*, but now they could find the opportunity to start the fire peacefully. Being forbidden to offer sacrifices, the *Brahmans* were very distressed in mind, intelligence and activities, but just on the point of Krishna's appearance, automatically their minds became full of joy because they could hear loud vibrations in the sky of transcendental sounds proclaiming the appearance of the Supreme Personality of Godhead.

The denizens of the Gandharva and Kinnara planets began to sing, and the denizens of Siddhaloka and the planets of the Caranas began to offer prayers in the service of the Personality of Godhead. In the heavenly planets, the angels along with their wives, accompanied by the Apsaras, began to dance. The great sages and the demigods, being pleased, began to shower flowers. At the seashore, there was the sound of mild waves, and above the sea there were clouds in the sky which began to thunder very pleasingly.

When things were adjusted like this,[4] Lord Vishnu, who is residing within the heart of every living entity, appeared in the darkness of night as the Supreme Personality of Godhead before Devaki, who also appeared as one of the demigoddesses. The appearance of Lord Vishnu at that time could be compared with the full moon in the sky as it rises on the eastern horizon. The objection may be raised that, since Lord Krishna appeared on the eighth day of the waning moon, there could be no rising of the full moon. In answer to this it may be said that Lord Krishna appeared in the dynasty which is in the hierarchy of the moon; therefore, although the moon was incomplete on that night, because of the Lord's appearance in the dynasty wherein the moon is himself the original person, the moon was in an overjoyous condition, so by the grace of Krishna he could appear just as a full moon.

Vasudeva saw that wonderful child born as a baby with four hands, holding conch shell, club, disc, and lotus flower, decorated with the mark of Srivatsa,[5] wearing the jeweled necklace of *kaustubha*[6] stone, dressed in yellow silk, appearing dazzling like a bright blackish cloud, wearing a helmet bedecked with the *vaidurya*[7] stone, valuable bracelets, earrings and similar other ornaments all over His body and an abundance of hair on His head. Due to the extraordinary features of the child, Vasudeva was struck with wonder. How could a newly born child be so decorated? He could therefore understand that Lord Krishna had now appeared, and he became overpowered by the occasion. Vasudeva very humbly wondered that although he was an ordinary living entity conditioned by material nature and was externally imprisoned by Kamas, the all-pervading Personality of Godhead, Vishnu or Krishna, was appearing as a child in his home, exactly in His original position. No earthly child is born with four hands decorated with ornaments and nice clothing, fully equipped with all the signs of the Supreme Personality of Godhead. Over and over again, Vasudeva glanced at his child, and he considered how to celebrate this auspicious moment: "Generally, when a male child is born," he thought, "people observe the occasion with jubilant celebrations, and in my home, although I am imprisoned, the Supreme Personality of Godhead has taken birth. How many millions of millions of times should I be prepared to observe this auspicious ceremony!"

When Vasudeva, who is also called Anakadundubhi, was looking at his newborn baby, he was so happy that he wanted to give many thousands of cows in charity to the *brahmanas*. According to the Vedic system, whenever there is an auspicious ceremony in the *ksatriya*[8] king's palace, the king gives many things in charity. Cows decorated with golden ornaments are delivered to the *brahmanas* and sages. Vasudeva wanted to perform a charitable ceremony to celebrate Krishna's appearance, but because he was shackled within the walls of Kamsa's prison, this was not possible. Instead, within his mind he gave thousands of cows to the *brahmanas*.

When Vasudeva was convinced that the newborn child was the Supreme Personality of Godhead Himself, he bowed down with folded hands and began to offer Him prayers. At that time Vasudeva was in the transcendental position, and he became completely free from all fear of Kamas. The newborn baby was also flashing His effulgence within the room in which He appeared. Vasudeva then began to offer his prayers. "My dear Lord, I can understand who You are. You are the Supreme Personality of

Godhead, the Super soul of all living entities and the Absolute Truth. You have appeared in Your own eternal form which is directly perceived by us. I understand that because I am afraid of Kamas, You have appeared just to deliver me from that fear. You do not belong to this material world; You are the same person who brings about the cosmic manifestation simply by glancing over material nature."

One may argue that the Supreme Personality of Godhead, who creates the whole cosmic manifestation simply by His glance, cannot come within the womb of Devaki, the wife of Vasudeva. To eradicate this argument, Vasudeva said, "My dear Lord, it is not a very wonderful thing that You appear within the womb of Devaki because the creation was also made in that way. You were lying in the Causal Ocean as Maha-Visnu, and by Your breathing process, innumerable universes came into existence. Then You entered into each of the universes as Garbhodakasayi Vishnu.[9] Then again You expanded Yourself as Ksirodakasayi Vishnu and entered into the hearts of all living entities and entered even within the atoms. Therefore Your entrance in the womb of Devaki is understandable in the same way. You appear to have entered, but You are simultaneously all-pervading. We can understand Your entrance and nonentrance from material examples. The total material energy remains intact even after being divided into sixteen elements. The material body is nothing but the combination of the five gross elements—namely earth, water, fire, air and ether. Whenever there is a material body, it appears that such elements are newly created, but actually the elements are always existing outside of the body. Similarly, although You appear as a child in the womb of Devaki, You are also existing outside. You are always in Your abode, but still You can simultaneously expand Yourself into millions of forms.

"One has to understand Your appearance with great intelligence because the material energy is also emanating from You. You are the original source of the material energy, just as the sun is the source of the sunshine. The sunshine cannot cover the sun globe, nor can the material energy—being an emanation from You—cover You. You appear to be in the three modes of material energy, but actually the three modes of material energy cannot cover You. This is understood by the highly intellectual philosophers. In other words, although You appear to be within the material energy, You are never covered by it."

"We hear from the Vedic version that the Supreme Brahman exhibits His effulgence, and therefore everything becomes illuminated. We can understand from *Brahma-samhita* that the *brahmajyoti*,[10] or the Brahman effulgence, emanates from the body of the Supreme Lord. And from the Brahman effulgence, all creation takes place. It is further stated in the Bhagavad-Gita that the Lord is also the support of the Brahman effulgence. Originally He is the root cause of everything. But persons who are less intelligent think that when the Supreme Personality of Godhead comes within this material world, He accepts the material qualities. Such conclusions are not very mature, but are made by the less intelligent.

"The Supreme Personality of Godhead is directly and indirectly existing everywhere; He is outside this material creation, and He is also within it. He is within this material creation not only as

Garbhodakasayi Vishnu; He is also within the atom. Existence is due to His presence. Nothing can be separated from His existence. In the Vedic injunction we find that the Supreme Soul or the root cause of everything has to be searched out because nothing exists independent of the Supreme Soul. Therefore the material manifestation is also a transformation of His potency. Both inert matter and the living force — soul — are emanations from 'Him. Only the foolish conclude that when the Supreme Lord appears He accepts the conditions of matter. Even if He appears to have accepted the material body, He is still not subjected to any material condition. Krishna has therefore appeared and defeated all imperfect conclusions about the appearance and disappearance of the Supreme Personality of Godhead.

"My Lord, Your appearance, existence and disappearance are beyond the influence of the material qualities. Because Your Lordship is the controller of everything and the resting place of the Supreme Brahman, there is nothing inconceivable or contradictory in You. As You have said, material nature works under Your superintendence. It is just like government officers working under the orders of the chief executive. The influence of subordinate activities cannot affect You. The Supreme Brahman and all phenomena are existing within You, and all the activities of material nature are controlled by Your Lordship.

"You are called *suklam. Suklam,* or 'whiteness' is the symbolic representation of the Absolute Truth because it is unaffected by the material qualities. Lord Brahma is called *rakta,* or red, because Brahma represents the qualities of passion for creation. Darkness is entrusted to Lord Siva[11] because he annihilates the cosmos. The creation, annihilation, and maintenance of this cosmic manifestation is conducted by Your potencies, yet You are always unaffected by those qualities. As confirmed in the *Vedas, harir hi nirgunah saksat:* the Supreme Personality of Godhead is always free from all material qualities. It is also said that the qualities of passion and ignorance are nonexistent in the person of the Supreme Lord.

"My Lord, You are the supreme controller, the Personality of Godhead, the supreme great, maintaining the order of this cosmic manifestation. And in spite of Your being the supreme controller, You have so kindly appeared in my home. The purpose of Your appearance is to kill the followers of the demoniac rulers of the world who are in the dress of royal princes but are actually demons. I am sure that You will kill all of them and their followers and soldiers."

Author's note: Vasudeva and Devaki, Krishna's parents, were imprisoned because Kamas, an evil king (Krishna's uncle), heard a voice that told him Devaki's eighth child would kill him.

"I understand that You have appeared to kill the uncivilized Kamas and his followers. But knowing that You were to appear to kill him and his followers, he has already killed so many of Your predecessors, elder brothers. Now he is simply awaiting the news of Your birth. As soon as he hears about it, he will immediately appear with all kinds of weapons to kill You."

After this prayer of Vasudeva, Devaki, the mother of Krishna, offered her prayers. She was very frightened because of her brother's atrocities. Devaki said, "My dear Lord, Your eternal forms, like Narayana, Lord Rama, Sesa, Varaha, Nrsimha, Vamana, Baladeva, and millions of similar incarnations emanating from Vishnu, are described in the Vedic literature as original. You are original because all Your forms as incarnations are outside of this material creation. Your form was existing before this cosmic manifestation was created. Your forms are eternal and all-pervading. They are self-effulgent, changeless and uncontaminated by the material qualities. Such eternal forms are ever-cognizant and full of bliss; they are situated in transcendental goodness and are always engaged in different pastimes. You are not limited to a particular form only; all such transcendental eternal forms are self-sufficient. I can understand that You are the Supreme Lord Vishnu ...

"My Lord, I offer my respectful obeisances unto You because You are the director of the unmanifested total energy, and the ultimate reservoir of the material nature. My Lord, the whole cosmic manifestation is under the influence of time, beginning from the moment up to the duration of the year. All act under Your direction. You are the original director of everything and the reservoir of all potent energies.

"Therefore my Lord, I request You to save me from the cruel hands of the son of Ugrasena, Kamas. I am praying to Your Lordship to please rescue me from this fearful condition because You are always ready to give protection to Your servitors." The Lord has confirmed this statement in the Bhagavad-Gita by assuring Arjuna, "You may declare to the world, My devotee shall never be vanquished."

While thus praying to the Lord for rescue, mother Devaki expressed her motherly affection: "I understand that this transcendental form is generally perceived in meditation by the great sages, but I am still afraid because as soon as Kamsa understands that You have appeared, he might harm You. So I request that for the time being You become invisible to our material eyes." In other words, she requested the Lord to assume the form of an ordinary child. "My only cause of fear from my brother Kamsa is due to Your appearance. My Lord Madhusudana, Kamsa may know that You are already born. Therefore I request You to conceal this four-armed form of Your Lordship which holds the four symbols of Vishnu—namely the conch shell, the disc, the club and the lotus flower. My dear Lord, at the end of the annihilation of the cosmic manifestation, You put the whole universe within Your abdomen; still by Your unalloyed mercy You have appeared in my womb. I am surprised that You imitate the activities of ordinary human beings just to please Your devotee."

On hearing the prayers of Devaki, the Lord replied, "My dear mother, in the millennium of Svayambhuva Manu,[12] My father Vasudeva was living as one of the *Prajapatis*, and his name at that time was Sutapa, and you were his wife named Prsni. At that time, when Lord Brahma was desiring to increase the population, he requested you to generate offspring. You controlled your senses and performed severe austerities. By practicing the breathing exercise of the *yoga* system, both you and your husband could tolerate all the influences of the material laws: the rainy season, the onslaught of the wind, and the scorching heat of the sunshine. You also executed all religious principles. In this way you were able to cleanse your heart and control the influence of material law. In executing your austerity, you used to eat only the leaves of the trees which fell to the ground. Then with steady mind and controlled sex drive, you worshiped Me, desiring some wonderful benediction from Me. Both of you practiced severe austerities for twelve thousand years, by the calculation of the demigods. During that time, your mind was always absorbed in Me. When you were executing devotional service and always thinking of Me within your heart, I was very much pleased with you. O sinless mother, your heart is therefore always pure. At that time also I appeared before you in this form just to fulfill your desire, and I asked you to ask whatever you desired. At that time you wished to have Me born as your son. Although you saw Me personally, instead of asking for your complete liberation from the material bondage, under the influence of My energy, you asked Me to become your son."

In other words, the Lord selected His mother and father—namely Prsni and Sutapa—specifically to appear in the material world. Whenever the Lord comes as a human being, He must have someone as a mother and father, so He selected Prsni and Sutapa perpetually as His mother and father. And on account of this, both Prsni and Sutapa could not ask the Lord for liberation. Liberation is not so important as the transcendental loving service of the Lord. The Lord could have awarded Prsni and Sutapa immediate liberation, but He preferred to keep them within this material world for His different appearances, as will be explained in the following verses. On receiving the benediction from the Lord to become His father and mother, both Prsni and Sutapa returned from the activities of austerity and lived as husband and wife in order to beget a child who was the Supreme Lord Himself.

In due course of time Prsni became pregnant and gave birth to the child. The Lord spoke to Devaki and Vasudeva: "At that time My name was Prsnigarbha. In the next millennium also you took birth as Aditi and Kasyapa, and I became your child of the name Upendra. At that time My form was just like a dwarf, and for this reason I was known as Vamanadeva. I gave you the benediction that I would take birth as your son three times. The first time I was known as Prsnigarbha, born of Prsni and Sutapa, the next birth I was Upendra born of Aditi and Kasyapa, and now for the third time I am born as Krishna from you, Devaki and Vasudeva. I appeared in this Vishnu form just to convince you that I am the same Supreme Personality of Godhead again taken birth. I could have appeared just like an ordinary child, but in that way you would not believe that I, the Supreme Personality of Godhead, have taken birth in your womb. My dear father and mother, you have therefore raised Me many times as your child, with great affection and love, and I am therefore very pleased and obliged to you. And I assure you that this time you shall go back to home, back to Godhead, on account of your perfection in your mission. I know you are very concerned about Me and afraid of Kamas. Therefore I order you to take Me immediately to Gokula [sic] and replace Me with the daughter who has just been born to Yasoda."

Having spoken thus in the presence of His father and mother, the Lord turned Himself into an ordinary child and remained silent. Being ordered by the Supreme Personality of Godhead, Vasudeva attempted to take his son from the delivery room, and exactly at that time, a daughter was born of Nanda and Yasoda. She was *Yogamaya*, the internal potency of the Lord. By the influence of this internal potency, *Yogamaya*,[13] all the residents of Kamsa's palace, especially the doorkeepers, were overwhelmed with deep sleep, and all the palace doors opened, although they were barred and shackled with iron chains. The night was very dark, but as soon as Vasudeva took Krishna on his lap and went out, he could see everything just as in the sunlight.

In the *Caitanya-caritamrta* it is said that Krishna is just like sunlight, and wherever there is Krishna, the illusory energy, which is compared to darkness, cannot remain. When Vasudeva was carrying Krishna, the darkness of the night disappeared. All the prison doors automatically opened. At the same time there was a thunder in the sky and severe rainfall. While Vasudeva was carrying his son Krishna in the falling rain, Lord Sesa in the shape of a serpent spread His hood over the head of Vasudeva so that he would not be hampered by the rainfall. Vasudeva came onto the bank of the Yamuna and saw that the water of the Yamuna was roaring with waves and that the whole span was full of foam. Still, in that furious feature, the river gave passage to Vasudeva to cross, just as the great Indian Ocean gave a path to Lord Rama[14] when He was bridging over the gulf. In this way Vasudeva crossed the river Yamuna. On the other side, he went to the place of Nanda Maharaja situated in Gokula, where he saw that all the cowherd men were fast asleep. He took the opportunity of silently entering into the house of Yasoda, and without difficulty he replaced his son, taking away the baby girl newly born in the house of Yasoda. Then, after entering the house very silently and exchanging the boy with the girl, he again returned to the prison of Kamas and silently put the girl on the lap of Devaki. He again clamped the shackles on himself so that

Kamas could not recognize that so many things had happened.

Mother Yasoda understood that a child was born of her, but because she was very tired from the labor of childbirth, she was fast asleep. When she awoke, she could not remember whether she had given birth to a male or a female child.

This ends the description of Krishna's appearance.

Krishna's disappearance is taken from the Srimad Bhagavatam, canto 1, chapter 14:

Sri Suta Gosvami said: "Arjuna went to Dvaraka to see Lord Sri Krishna and other friends and also to learn from the Lord of His next activities. A few months passed, and Arjuna did not return."

Maharaja Yudhishthira then began to observe some inauspicious omens, which were fearful in themselves. He saw that the direction of eternal time had changed, and this was very fearful. There were disruptions in the seasonal regularities. The people in general had become very greedy, angry and deceitful. And he saw that they were adopting foul means of livelihood. All ordinary transactions and dealings became polluted with cheating, even between friends. And in familial affairs, there was always misunderstanding between fathers, mothers and sons, between well-wishers, and between brothers. Even between husband and wife there was always strain and quarrel.

In course of time it came to pass that people in general became accustomed to greed, anger, pride, etc. Maharaja Yudhishthira, observing all these omens, spoke to his younger brother, Bhimasena, "I sent Arjuna to Dvaraka to meet his friends and to learn from the Personality of Godhead Krishna of His program of work. Since he departed, seven months have passed, yet he has not returned. I do not know factually how things are going there. Is He going to quit His earthly pastimes, as Devarshi indicated? Has that time already arrived? From Him only, all our kingly opulence, good wives, lives, progeny, control over our subjects, victory over our enemies, and future accommodations in higher planets have become possible. All this is due to His causeless mercy upon us. Just see, O man with a tiger's strength, how many miseries due to celestial influences, earthly reactions and bodily pains — all very dangerous in themselves — are foreboding danger in the near future by deluding our intelligence. The left side of my body, my thighs, arms and eyes are all quivering again and again. I am having heart palpitations due to fear. All this indicates undesirable happenings. Just see, O Bhima, how the she jackal cries at the rising sun and vomits fire, and how the dog barks at me fearlessly. O Bhimasena, tiger amongst men, now useful animals like cows are passing me on my left side, and lower animals like the asses are circumambulating me. My horses appear to weep upon seeing me. Just see! This pigeon is like a messenger of death. The shrieks of the owls and their rival crows make my heart tremble. It appears that they want to make a void of the whole universe. Just see how the smoke encircles the sky. It appears that the earth and mountains are throbbing. Just hear the cloudless thunder and see the bolts from the blue. The wind blows violently, blasting dust everywhere and creating darkness. Clouds are raining everywhere with bloody disasters. The rays of the sun are declining, and the stars appear to be fighting amongst themselves. Confused living entities appear to be ablaze and weeping. Rivers, tributaries, ponds, reservoirs and the mind are all perturbed. Butter no longer ignites fire.

"What is this extraordinary time? What is going to happen? The calves do not suck the teats of the cows, nor do the cows give milk. They are standing, crying, tears in their eyes, and the bulls take no pleasure in the pasturing grounds. The Deities seem to be crying in the temple, lamenting and perspiring. They seem about to leave. All the cities, villages, towns, gardens, mines and hermitages are now devoid of beauty and bereft of all happiness. I do not know what sort of calamities are now awaiting us. I think that all these earthly disturbances indicate some greater loss to the good fortune of the world. The world was fortunate to have been marked with the footprints of the lotus feet of the Lord. These signs indicate that this will no longer be."

O Brahmana Saunaka, while Maharaja Yudishthira, observing the inauspicious signs on the earth at that time, was thus thinking to himself, Arjuna came back from the city of the Yadus [Dvaraka]. When he bowed at his feet, the King saw that his dejection was unprecedented. His head was down, and tears glided from his lotus eyes. Seeing Arjuna pale due to heartfelt anxieties, the King, remembering the indications of the sage Narada, questioned him in the midst of friends.

Maharaja Yudhisthira said: "My dear brother, please tell me whether our friends and relatives, such as Madhu, Bhoja, Dasarha, Arha, Satvata, Andhaka and the members of the Yadu family are all passing their days in happiness. Is my respectable grandfather Surasena in a happy mood? And are my maternal uncle Vasudeva and his younger brothers all doing well? His seven wives, headed by Devaki, are all sisters. Are they and their sons and daughters-in-law all happy? Are Ugrasena, whose son was the mischievous Kamas, and his younger brother still living? Are Hridika and his son Kritavarma happy? Are Akura, Javanta, Gada, Sarana, and Satrujit all happy? How is Balarama, the Personality of Godhead and the protector of devotees? How is Pradyumna, the great general of the Vrishni family? Is He happy? And is Aniruddha, the plenary expansion of the Personality of Godhead, faring well? Are all the chieftain sons of Lord Krishna, such as Sushena, Carudeshna, Samba the son of Jambavati, and Rishabha, along with their sons, all doing well? Also, Srutadeva, Uddhava and others, Nanda, Sunanda and other leaders of liberated souls who are constant companions of the Lord are protected by Lord Balarama and Krishna. Are they all doing well in their respective functions? Do they, who are all eternally bound in friendship with us, remember our welfare? Is Lord Krishna, the Supreme Personality of Godhead, who gives pleasure to the cows, the senses and the brahmanas[sic], who is very affectionate towards His devotees, enjoying the pious assembly at Dvaraka Puri surrounded by friends?

"The original Personality of Godhead, the enjoyer, and Balarama, the primeval Lord Ananta, are staying in the ocean of the Yadu dynasty for the welfare, protection and general progress of the entire universe. And the members of the Yadu dynasty, being protected by the arms of the Lord, are enjoying life like the residents of the spiritual sky. Simply by administering comforts at the lotus feet of the Lord, which is the most important of all services, the queens at Dvaraka, headed by Satyabhama, induced the Lord to conquer the demigods. Thus the queens enjoy things which are prerogatives of the wives of the controller of thunderbolts. The great heroes of the Yadu dynasty, being protected by the arms of Lord Sri Krishna, always remain fearless in every respect. And therefore their feet trample over the Sudharma assembly house, which the best demigods deserved but which was taken away from them. My brother Arjuna, please tell me whether your health is all right. You appear to have lost your bodily luster. Is this due to others disrespecting and neglecting you because of your long stay at Dvaraka? Has someone addressed you with unfriendly words or threatened you? Could you not give charity to one who asked, or could you not keep your promise to someone? You are always the protector of the deserving living beings, such as brahmanas, children, cows, women and the diseased. Could you not give them protection when they approached you for shelter? Have you contacted a woman of impeachable character, or have you not properly treated a deserving woman? Or have you been defeated on the way by someone who is inferior or equal to you? Have you not taken care of old men and boys who deserve to dine with you? Have you left them and taken your meals alone? Have you committed some unpardonable mistake which is considered to be abominable? Or is it that you are feeling empty for all time because you might have lost your most intimate friend, Lord Krishna? O my brother Arjuna, I can think of no other reason for your becoming so dejected."

Again in the Srimad Bhagavatam, a description is given of Lord Krishna's disappearance in canto 11, chapter 31: The Disappearance of Lord Sri Krishna:

Sukadeva Gosvāmī said: "Then Lord Brahma arrived at Prabhāsa along with Lord Siva and his consort, the sages, the Prajāpatis and all the demigods, headed by Indra. The forefathers, Siddhas, Gandharvas, Vidyādharas and great serpents also came, along with the Cāraṇas, Yakṣas, Rākṣasas, Kinnaras, Apsarās and relatives of Garuda, greatly eager to witness the departure of the Supreme Personality of Godhead. As they were coming, all these personalities variously chanted and glorified the birth and activities of Lord Sauri [Krishna]. O King, crowding the sky with their many airplanes,[15] they showered down flowers with great devotion.

"Seeing before Him Brahma, the grandfather of the universe, along with the other demigods, who are all His personal and powerful expansions, the Almighty Lord closed His lotus eyes, fixing His mind within Himself, the Supreme Personality of Godhead. Without employing the mystic āgneyī meditation to burn up His transcendental body, which is the all-attractive resting place of all the worlds and the object of all contemplation and meditation, Lord Krishna entered into His own abode.

"As soon as Lord Sri Krishna left the earth, Truth, Religion, Faithfulness, Glory and Beauty immediately followed Him. Kettledrums resounded in the heavens and flowers showered from the sky. Most of the demigods and other higher beings led by Brahma could not see Lord Krishna as He was entering His own abode, since He did not reveal His movements. But some of them did catch sight of Him, and they were extremely amazed. Just as ordinary men cannot ascertain the path of a lightning bolt as it leaves a cloud, the demigods could not trace out the movements of Lord Krishna as He returned to His abode. A few of the demigods, however—notably Lord Brahma and Lord Siva—could ascertain how the Lord's mystic power was working, and thus they became astonished. All the demigods praised the Lord's mystic power and then returned to their own planets.

"'My dear King, (Pariksit) you should understand that the Supreme Lord's appearance and disappearance, which resemble those of embodied conditioned souls, are actually a show enacted by His illusory energy, just like the performance of an actor. After creating this universe He enters into it, plays within it for some time, and at last winds it up. Then the Lord remains situated in His own transcendental glory, having ceased from the functions of cosmic manifestation. Lord Krishna brought the son of His guru back from the planet of the lord of death in the boy's selfsame body, and as the ultimate giver of protection He saved you also when you were burned by the brahmastra of Asvatthama. He conquered in battle even Lord Siva, who deals death to the agents of death, and He sent the hunter Jara directly to Vaikuntha in his human body. How could such a personality be unable to protect His own Self?'"

Although Lord Krishna, being the possessor of infinite powers, is the only cause of the creation, maintenance and destruction of innumerable living beings, He simply did not desire to keep His body in this world any longer. Thus He revealed the destination of those fixed in the self and demonstrated that this mortal world is of no intrinsic value.

Anyone who regularly rises early in the morning and carefully chants with devotion the glories of Lord Sri Krishna's transcendental disappearance and His return to His own abode will certainly achieve that same supreme destination. As soon as Daruka reached Dvaraka, he threw himself at the feet of Vasudeva and Ugrasena and drenched their feet with his tears, lamenting the loss of Lord Krishna. Daruka delivered the account of the total destruction of the Vṛṣṇis, and upon hearing this, O Pariksit, the people became deeply distraught in their hearts and stunned with sorrow. Feeling the overwhelming pain of separation from Krishna, they struck their own faces while hurrying to the place where their relatives lay dead.

When Devaki, Rohini and Vasudeva could not find their sons, Krishna and Rama, they lost consciousness out of anguish. Tormented by separation from the Lord, His parents gave up their lives at that very spot.

"My dear Pariksit, the wives of the Yādavas then climbed onto the funeral pyres, embracing their dead husbands. The wives of Lord Balara (Krishna's Brother) also entered the fire and embraced His body, and Vasudeva's wives entered his fire and embraced his body. The daughters-in-law of Lord Hari entered the funeral fires of their respective husbands, headed by Pradyumna. And Rukmini and the other wives of Lord Krishna—whose hearts were completely absorbed in Him—entered His fire.

"Arjuna felt great distress over separation from Lord Krishna, his dear most friend. But he consoled himself by remembering the transcendental words the Lord had sung to him. Arjuna then saw to it that the funeral rites were properly carried out for the dead, who had no remaining male family members. He executed the required ceremonies for each of the Yadus, one after another.

"As soon as Dvaraka was abandoned by the Supreme Personality of Godhead, the ocean flooded it on all sides, O King, sparing only His palace.

Lord Madhusudana [sic], the Supreme Personality of Godhead, is eternally present in Dvaraka. It is the most auspicious of all auspicious places, and merely remembering it destroys all contamination.

"Arjuna took the survivors of the Yadu dynasty — the women, children and old men — to Indraprastha, where he installed Vajra as ruler of the Yadus. Hearing from Arjuna of the death of their friend, my dear King, your grandfathers established you as the maintainer of the dynasty and left to prepare for their departure from this world. A person who with faith engages in chanting the glories of these various pastimes and incarnations of Vishnu, the Lord of lords, will gain liberation from all sins. The all-auspicious exploits of the all-attractive incarnations of Lord Sri Krishna, the Supreme Personality of Godhead, and also the pastimes He performed as a child, are described in this Srimad-Bhagavatam and in other scriptures. Anyone who clearly chants these descriptions of His pastimes will attain transcendental loving service unto Lord Krishna, who is the goal of all perfect sages."

This ends the description of Lord Sri Krishna's departure from this material world.

You can see from the descriptions given here how dear Lord Sri Krishna was to every one of his personal acquaintances. When he left, they all felt no reason to live. Such is the power of the presence of God. Once you've been in that presence, you never want to leave. Once he leaves, you don't want to live. This is called separation. All our problems can be looked at as evidence of our separation from God, because in his presence we experience everything good we could ever hope for. Without him we can do nothing. Two things to do: 1. Always remember him, and 2. Never forget him.

To experience him here now, he gives a scientific process. His most recent incarnation as a devotee named Caitanya is called Maha Prabhu because he is the Great Master. He gives the understanding that in this age, because of the nature of the fallen souls, he establishes the means of returning to him as the chanting of his holy names. By chanting with a pure heart, with no expectation of anything in return, one can develop a taste for love of God and thereby become purified enough to enter the spiritual world at the end of this life. His original instructions are: *Hare nama, hare nama, hare nama eva kevalam, kalau nasty eva, nasty eva, nasty eva, gatir unyatah,* which translated means: "the holy names, the holy names, the holy names, there is no other way, there is no other way, there is no other way in this age of kali, therefore chant constantly." This chanting can be done anywhere, even silently within the mind. This is the great (Maha) mantra for deliverance. Hare Krishna, Hare Krishna, Krishna, Krishna, Hare, Hare, Hare Rama, Hare Rama, Rama, Rama Hare, Hare. If you will take up this chanting every day, you will agree, nothing is so sublime as the taste of the nectar of the holy names of God!

Notes:

1. Rohini (taken from blogspot.com), known as Aldebaran, is something special. It cannot be missed in the autumn sky where the trapezium-shaped Orion is a feast to the eyes. Rohini lies close to Orion, but it is part of the constellation Taurus, the bull. The V shape of the bull's face cannot be missed, with a bright and orange-tinted Rohini in one of the arms of the V-shaped formation of stars.
2. Brahma: In Vedic texts, Brahma is recognized as the firstborn of the universe.
3. Brahman: The Brahmans are the priestly class who perform sacrifices in the temple for the pleasure of the Supreme Lord.
4. Lord Vishnu: In the heart of every living being, an expansion of the Supreme Lord is manifest. He is also called Paramatma or the super soul.

5. Srivatsa: A lock of hair on the right side of Sri Vishnu's chest (the creative Body of Sri Krishna).
6. Kaustabha: The most precious stone kept by the Supreme Lord.
7. Vaidūrya: The same term is used to designate a special diamond; sometimes lapis lazuli and sometimes an emerald.
8. Ksatriya: The Ksatriya class administers justice in the form of creating laws, a militia, and in general the governing class.
9. Gharbodaksayi Vishnu: An expansion of the supreme as the origin of the material universe, who lies on the Gharbodak Ocean.
10. Brahmajyoti: The effulgence of the Supreme Lord, sought by impersonalist spiritualists who believe God's energy is greater than God the person. Their ultimate goal is to merge into this effulgence, as compared to the bhaktas, who aspire after the service of their God.
13. Yogamaya: The illusory energy of God that keeps Krishna's intimate associates from knowing he is God, for the sake of them being able to conduct their lives as parents, friends, lovers, etc. of Krishna. Without Yogamaya, Krishna would not be able to have intimate association, as everyone would be in awe of him. Krishna likes intimate relationships with his devotees.
14. Lord Rama: An incarnation of Krishna who appeared many millennia ago as a perfect king. The "Ramayana" is the ancient Indian classic writing describing the life and pastimes of Lord Ram.
15. Airplanes: Although this records an event that took place five thousand years ago, airplanes are described as being present. There is an entire scripture called the vamana sastra that describes in detail how such airplanes are made. Interpretation is left (in this age) to the reader, however.

# Hinduism

Hinduism is a diverse religion. It is not made up of many deities but of different aspects of the same deity, Brahma. Brahma is called the creator and is considered the supreme and absolute deity. The two other fundamental deities of Hinduism are Vishnu, the preserver, and Shiva, the destroyer. Other themes that can be found in all forms of Hinduism are: "Dharma, ethics and duties; Samsara, rebirth; Karma, the right actions and Moksha, the liberation from the birth, death and rebirth sequence."[11] Hinduism also believes in honesty, truth, austerity, perseverance, nonviolence, contentment, cleanliness, prayers, penance, and pious company. "The major and most popular Hindu texts include the Bhagavad-Gita, the Upanishads, and the epics of Ramayana and Mahabharata."[12]

## An Interview with Dr. Yash Lakra

### With Excerpts from *Real Questions about Hinduism* by the Hindu American Foundation

I was introduced to Dr. Yash Lakra in a Hindu temple by Avinash and Sema Shah (who I met at a Jain temple). Yash Lakra, an elder in the temple, was kind enough to meet with me a few times and gave me the book *Real Questions about Hinduism*. His explanation of "Who is God," according to the Hindu faith, was very enlightening. The hospitality offered by Dr. Lakra and his wife was superb. Not

---

[11] "The Main Tenets of Hinduism: Hinduism for Beginners," www.hinduism. about.com/od/basics/p/hinduismbasics.htm.

[12] Ibid.

only are they excellent hosts, but Mrs. Lakra is also a wonderful artist.

The concept of God in Hinduism is much different than the concept of God in other major religions. We call this concept Brahman. Brahman is formless, shapeless, has no name, has no beginning and no end, never was born or dies, and cannot be divided. Brahman, which is shapeless, can will itself to take a form or shape and can also will itself to be born.

Brahman can be divided into three personalities called Brahma, Vishnu, and Shiva. Brahma is the creator, Vishnu is the sustainer and is responsible for sustaining the creation, and Shiva is the destroyer. The reason for Shiva is whatever is created ultimately has to be destroyed for the rejuvenation of the new; in other words, old things have to change for new things to come. This trinity is a division of three aspects of the same divinity.

Vishnu has incarnated on earth at various times in different forms. First was a turtle, then a fish, a wild boar, a beast made up of half lion and half man, a miniature or dwarf man, an angry fighting man, and then came Rama. Rama was a philosopher king, and he was the embodiment of all morality and ethical behavior. He set the example of how a son has to act, how a brother has to act, how a king has to act; in other words, how you create morality and ethical behavior in this world. Then Krishna came along, and he gave us the message of Bhagavad-Gita, the most followed religious book of the Hindus. The pattern we have for the incarnations follows evolution of life or creation in this world.

Many people call Hinduism a polytheistic religion because we have different gods with different names and shapes. But for us Hindus, there is only one god; the other manifestations are of the same god. In other words, the different forms, shapes, and names of different gods are manifestations of the same god, Brahman. That god or Brahman or consciousness prevails in the whole creation. So you see, God is everything. That is why we see divinity in everything. The creation is holy because it is a manifestation of the same creator. Therefore, Hinduism is not a polytheistic religion; it sees God in various forms and shapes. For every masculine form of God, we have a feminine form in order to complete the creation. Hinduism allows people the freedom to choose the form of God they feel comfortable in worshiping. Every god form is given certain attributes and qualities. Since God is omnipotent and can take any form, we have no problems. If a person wishes not to worship a particular form of God or worships God in various forms, there is no quarrel between people.

Now we come to how to worship God. Obviously no religion is complete or can exist without the concept of God and how to relate or pray to God. The word *pray* in Hinduism is called *yoga*. Our philosophers realized that every human being has different inclinations. Some people are the meditative type; they want to meditate. Some people don't believe in rituals; they want to do work without any expectations or rewards. This is called Karam yoga or path of action. Still others are the devotional types who wish to sing the praise of the Lord. We call this Bhakti yoga or path of devotion. Other individuals just want to read philosophy and think about it. This path of knowledge is called Giran yoga. The ways people relate to God depend on their own tendencies and inclinations.

As it relates to evil, we think there is probably a force as strong as God somewhere, and they are in a constant struggle. If someone is influenced by godly powers, that person is nice and good. If a person is influenced by devilish forces, that person is bad. Hinduism says there are no outside forces making you good or evil. In the book *Real Questions about Hinduism* by the Hindu American Foundation, it states:

> Because Hindus believe in karma and reincarnation, the concept of heaven and hell as worlds of eternal glory or damnation do not exist in Hinduism. Hindus also do not ascribe to the concept of Satan or devil that is in eternal opposition of God. Some Hindus believe in what is described in scriptures as

two planes of existence, svarga and naraka that can be likened to heaven and hell, respectively. Neither is permanent or eternal. Both are intermediary planes of existence in which the soul might exhaust a portion of its karmic debt or surplus before taking physical birth once again to strive for moksha.

The basic concept of Hinduism is that the world is a source of misery and suffering. You obtain freedom from this suffering by being born over and over again, depending on your karma, until you reach nirvana. The only way to achieve nirvana is through righteous work and ethical behavior. There are more than eight million forms of life you have to pass through in order to ultimately get human life. Human life gives you the best chance to free yourself from the cycle of death and birth. If you are not righteous, you may have to be born into another form of life and work your way to being born as a human again.

In Hinduism there are four objectives to life: dharma, artha, kama, and moksha. Dharma, the first objective, means that your behavior should be good, ethical, and righteous. Artha means that material wealth should be obtained by dharma behavior. Kama says that once you have created wealth, you should enjoy its pleasures, with the understanding that all of your actions have consequences.

From the book *Real Answers about Hinduism*:

> The ultimate purpose and goal for a Hindu's religious and spiritual practice is to attain moksha. Moksha is achieved through self-realization or realization of one's true divine nature. Hindus believe that each individual (anything living) is a divine soul, but that spiritual ignorance leads one to identify the self completely with the body and ego, therefore forgetting the divine nature of not only one's self but all of existence. Moksha is characterized by the overcoming of spiritual ignorance; the complete elimination of material desires and attachments; the

perfect ability to live in the present moment and experience absolute peace; and most importantly, the awakening of pure compassion towards all. Moksha also translates to liberation from the cycle of birth and rebirth. Someone may attain moksha during his or her lifetime or upon the death of his or her physical body.

# Humanistic Style Judaism

Humanistic Judaism was founded in 1969 and offers a nonreligious approach to Jewish culture and identity. One of the primary ethical activities of the religion is helping people assume responsibility for their own lives. Humanistic Judaism believes that people must be treated in a fair manner, with respect, and in a way that individuality and dignity are affirmed. It also focuses on rationality, personal autonomy, feminism, and mutual understanding and cooperation among all religions and philosophies of life.

## Finding a Spokesperson

I was having a conversation with the eminent attorney Benson Barr and mentioned that I was creating a book with different religious viewpoints and that part of my challenge was meeting leaders from different religions. He stated that his brother was a rabbi and may be interested in helping out on this project. A few days later, I received an e-mail from Benson Barr with his brother's phone number and website. I contacted Rabbi Robert Barr, and we had a discussion. Within that exchange, I told him that the book I was working on was about the divergent ways religions view God. Rabbi Barr, after listening intently, suggested that I use the liturgy that members of his temple had written. The liturgy answered the question I was asking. The following is the liturgy from Temple Beth Adam's Ritual / Life Committee, titled "God Concept."

## By Temple Beth Adam's Ritual / Life Cycle Committee

Jews throughout the ages have tried to understand God and God's relationship with their world. These questions are addressed in the Bible and Talmud and have been contemplated by many great Jewish thinkers, including Philo, Maimonides, Spinoza, and Kaplan. Thus, at Beth Adam, we carry on a tradition that was begun many centuries ago.

The concept of God has undergone constant modification in Judaism. The God of the prophets is different from the God of Abraham, Isaac, and Jacob; certainly the God of Maimonides is different from them both. It is impossible to examine here the myriad of concepts for the term *God*, for that would take volumes. Every Jewish thinker has suggested an understanding of the term, redefining how God interacts and participates in the affairs of the world. Many feminist theologians are trying to reconcile traditional male interpretations of God and modern feminist thought. There has always been and continues to be great diversity in the Jewish understanding of God.

Changes in theological concepts have never been readily accepted. Spinoza, whose theology was considered a heresy in his day, is today proclaimed by many as one of the greatest Jewish thinkers of all time. Over the years, ideas that were regarded as radical or heretical have come to be accepted by the community. Consequently, the entire spectrum of Jewish theology today is diverse and at times contradictory.

To be a Jew has never meant that one must accept some predefined concept of God. Each Jew has always had the right to understand the term as he or she determines. This is evidenced by the fact that the classic definition for the term *Jew*—one who is born of a Jewish mother or who converts according to traditional law—does not mention belief. It is clear from this definition that belief is not the primary factor in determining who is or is not a Jew. Lacking any definition of what one must believe to be a Jew, a Jew can accept any theological stand and still remain a Jew.

Because Beth Adam's services do not incorporate traditional prayers, many falsely assume that a humanistic approach to Judaism is atheistic. As acknowledged in our mission statement and reaffirmed in our educational philosophy, Beth Adam's liturgy "gives expression to Judaism's ever-evolving religious experience and promotes humanistic values of intellectual honesty, open inquiry, and human responsibility."

The understanding of Judaism does not preclude one's having a concept of God. In fact, there are many views of God that are compatible with this perspective. The basic criteria for determining whether a view of God is compatible with a humanistic perspective are whether it allows for the belief that the ultimate authority for what a person does rests with that individual and the belief that the events in our world are the product of human action and the laws of nature. At Beth Adam we also affirm that ethics and morals are the product of human thought and experience.

There are many members of Beth Adam who have a concept of God, but not a God that intervenes or manipulates the events of this world. Such a God does not hand down, dictate, or decree and does not regulate or direct the actions of human beings. Neither would this God act in a way that would contradict or be inconsistent with the laws of nature or scientific truth. Traditional prayer, which presupposes a God who intervenes in and manipulates the affairs of the world, is contrary to the worldview; thus, the use of such prayer in service would be incompatible with such a theological system. Individuals who have a concept of God affirm their Jewish identities in services that focus upon human beings' strengths and weaknesses, hopes and fears, pasts and futures. They recognize that traditional prayer is not essential for declaring one's membership with the Jewish people and that a service can affirm both their worldview and their Jewish identity.

Of course, there are those individuals who do not accept a concept of God at all; the term *God* does not reflect their views or attitudes about the world. However, they affirm their Jewish identities and their right and responsibility to control their own destinies based upon ethics and morals arising out of the human experience. Their desire to participate as Jews in a service that reflects their views is possible only in a congregation such as Beth Adam.

Whether or not an individual has a concept of God is not the central issue. What is central to Beth Adam is our agreement upon a philosophic system that is based upon human reason and experience. One's Jewish identity is a function of one's commitment to the Jewish people. Through public acts or statements, individuals declare their membership in the Jewish community.

The removal of specific language from the liturgy that invokes God does not preclude examination and discussion of concepts of God in other congregational settings; nor does it necessarily mean that the concept of God is not explored in services themselves. The fact is that the issue of God is addressed often and in depth. Once the concept of God becomes open to question and discussion, people feel free to express and examine ideas.

At Beth Adam, no one is judged based upon his or her theological system. Consequently, God is discussed, examined, questioned, and explored with an open and inquiring mind. Some may find this endeavor uncomfortable. They may prefer not to open the concept of God and God's role to discussion. But at Beth Adam, the ongoing search for truth and understanding is paramount. There is no issue too sacred to be discussed. The goal of Beth Adam is to enable people to work within our philosophic system to struggle and search for an understanding of the world in which they live, while affirming their Jewish identities.

# *Kabbalah*

Kabbalah was started by Hasidic Jews in Eastern Europe sometime in the 1700s. The basis of the religion is medieval Jewish mystical writings. By the 1780s this mystical writing was given a theoretical framework that is still used today. The writings state that all things are one with God, and there is no separation between the Creator and all things in the world. They also state that people should look at life in a joyous manner, because looking at life in a gloomy manner will not allow individuals to accept God's presence in the world.

## Finding a Spokesperson

In pursuit of a Kabbalist, I was fortunate enough to make the acquaintance of Karen Greenberg. In our phone conversation, Karen was extremely polite and offered to meet with me. At our encounter, Karen was intrigued by my project and offered to help. Karen is a warm and friendly individual who has an extreme amount of knowledge about the Kabbalist religion. For more than a decade, she has been traveling throughout the United States, teaching personal growth and the practical application of Universal Kabbalah. Karen has worked with people of all faiths. She has studied extensively with rabbis and teachers worldwide, has a degree in physical therapy, danced professionally, and owned her own dance studios. The following is Karen Greenberg's essay: "Who Is G-D? A Kabbalistic Perspective."

By Karen Greenberg

(*God* is written as *G-D* by some Jewish people out of reverence for the Holy One.)

G-D is beyond our human understanding. Any abstract conceptualization of G-D is insufficient, limited by our intellectual framework.

- G-D is the Source of all.
- The Source of everything is limitless, infinite, everywhere.
- The Source is timeless.
- The Source is eternal.
- It was. It is. It will be.
- The Source was always here, long before any of us was here.
- The Source will outlive us all.
- The Source is all-powerful.
- The Source is all-knowing.
- The Source is an enormous energy field, which is omnipresent, omnipotent, and omniscient.

The Source is *not uninvolved* with its inhabitants and this world. Rather, the Source is in everyone and in all that exists. Conversely, everyone and all that exists is in the Source. Just as a mother's umbilical cord (with her nutrients, oxygen, and waste removal) is inside her baby, and her baby is inside its mother, so it is with G-D. G-D is inside each of us, and we are inside of G-D. We are all of G-D's children. G-D cares about each and every one of His/Her children.

G-D is referred to as "His/Her" because in the Bible (the Torah / Old Testament), it says in Genesis, chapter 1, verses 26–27:

> And G-D said, "Let us make Man in Our image,
> After Our likeness.

They shall rule over the fish of the sea, the birds of the sky, and over the animals, the whole earth, and every creeping thing that creeps upon the earth."

So G-D created Man in His image, in the image of G-D he created him; Male and Female He created them.

G-D desires a personal relationship with each one of us. Some of us realize this and consult with G-D, perhaps several times throughout the day. This connection provides support, strength, and comfort, even in the most difficult times.

Conversely, others do not realize that G-D desires a personal relationship with them. They do not realize that G-D is inside of each one of us and we are inside of G-D. They are under the illusion that either there is no G-D, or that G-D created the world and then abandoned it and its people. The illusion that G-D does not exist or abandoned His creation can lead to disconnection, loneliness, depression, even despair and suicide.

If G-D was truly uninvolved, why did G-D bother to ask Adam's whereabouts in the garden of Eden after Adam and Eve partook of the fruit of the Tree of Knowledge of Good and Evil? See Genesis, chapter 3, verses 8–13:

They heard the sound of Hashem G-D manifesting itself in the garden toward evening; and the man and wife hid from Hashem G-D among the trees of the garden.

Hashem G-D called out to the man and said to him, "Where are you?"

He said, "I heard the sound of You in the garden, and I was afraid because I am naked, so I hid."

And He said, "Who told you that you are naked?

Have you eaten of the tree from which I commanded you not to eat?"

The man said, "The woman whom You gave to be with me—she gave me of the tree and I ate."

And Hashem G-D said to the woman, "What is this that you have done!"

The woman said, "The serpent deceived me, and I ate."

If G-D were uninvolved, then why would G-D give consequences to the serpent, Eve, and Adam? The serpent was to creep on its belly from now on, with enmity between the woman and him and all of their descendants. Secondly, Eve's offspring will pound the serpent's head, and the serpent will bite their heels. Additionally, Eve was to have pain in childbirth and would always yearn for closeness with her husband, but he would be elusive. Finally, Adam would have to work the soil for a living (rather than enjoying the free fruit from the Tree of Life), and practically all that he would reap would be thorns and thistles.

If G-D were not involved in this world, then why did G-D ask Cain his whereabouts and give consequences after Cain rose up against his brother, Abel, and killed him? See Genesis, chapter 4, verses 9–12:

Hashem said to Cain, "Where is Abel your brother?"

He said, "I don't know. Am I my brother's keeper?"

Hashem said, "What have you done? Your brother's blood is crying out to Me from the earth! Now, you are even more cursed than the ground, which opened its mouth to take your brother's blood from your hand! When you work the soil, it will no longer give its strength to you! You will be a wanderer over the earth!"

There are numerous occasions in the Torah / Old Testament / Bible, where G-D speaks to different characters, gives instructions, and enumerates blessings and negative consequences. G-D is definitely involved.

We have a free-will choice whether or not to develop our relationship with G-D. Some choose to develop a close relationship with G-D

- by connecting to the various names of G-D: Lord of the Earth, G-D Almighty, Deliverer, King, Elohim (Severity and Justice), Hashem (Merciful);
- by studying the Tree of Life from the garden of Eden in the first chapter of the Bible. Each part of the Tree of Life represents a different quality of our Creator. According to the Kabbalah, starting from the bottom of the tree and ascending, the following are the twelve parts of the Tree of Life:

1) *Malchut* – kingdom
2) *Yesod* – foundation
3) *Hod* – splendor
4) *Netzach* – victory
5) *Tiferet* – beauty
6) *Gevurah* – severity
7) *Chesed* – loving-kindness
8) *Da'at* – knowledge
9) *Binah* – understanding
10) *Chochmah* – wisdom
11) *Keter* – crown
12) *En-Sof* – source

By *studying* these, we become better acquainted with our Creator. By *embodying* these G-Dlike qualities, we become more like our Creator. By *emulating* these G-Dlike characteristics, we become more powerful creators. Once we have clarity regarding our "calling," we become more powerful cocreators (with G-D), of our souls' purposes. By fulfilling our souls' purposes, we can all do our particular portion of the great work and share the light of the Creator with each other, in order to create heaven on earth.

According to Rabbi Isaac Luria, a key contributor to the Kabbalistic system in the sixteenth century, in order for G-D to create the world, He/She had to contract to make space for material creation. In his emptiness, an *En Sofic* ray (of G-D's hidden essence) was inserted to create primordial man, the *Adam Kadmon*. The light from Adam Kadmon's eyes separated into different *sephirot* or spheres (G-Dlike qualities) or vessels in the Tree of Life. When these vessels were unable to contain all the light, they shattered. Most of the light returned to the Creator. However, some light attached to the broken shards. The shards were the shells for evil. The shards also were containers for the human souls who were contained within Adam's fall (when he partook of the fruit from the Tree of Knowledge of Good and Evil).

Each of us has a *tikkum* or correction to free both this light and these souls trapped in the evil shells, to elevate them, through prayer, performance of commandments with heartfelt intention, and through fulfilling our soul's purpose in joy and love. Then, this light and these trapped souls are liberated and elevated to return to the Unity of the Creator.

As we become more G-Dlike, we aspire to union with G-D. One of the ways to do so is to observe and practice the 613 commandments that are listed throughout the Torah / Old Testament / Bible. Many people are familiar with the Ten Commandments. However, scattered throughout the Old Testament, there are actually 613 commandments. (Some are not applicable today; some can only be performed in the Holy Land, the land of Israel, and others only if the Holy Temple in Jerusalem is standing. The temple was destroyed in the year 70 CE.) Two hundred forty-nine are positive commandments, for example, like commanding us to visit someone who is sick in the hospital; to provide hospitality in our homes for people who are seeking a place to stay; to bury the dead; to love G-D with all your heart, soul, and might; and so on.

Three hundred sixty-five are negative commandments. These include what we are prohibited from doing, such as having two different sets of weights and measures, a smaller one for *selling* to another individual, and a larger one for *buying* from another person. We are prohibited from working seven days per week and burning out.

Traditionally, as practicing Kabbalists, on the Sabbath (sundown Friday to sundown Saturday), we are prohibited from running errands; from cooking; from turning on the television, radio, computer, cell phone, car, stove, or oven. We are given time and space to talk to our spouses, our children, those in our community. We are given an opportunity to spend time with G-D, contemplating, meditating, reading, and praying, to commune with G-D and G-D's teachings. This is how we develop our relationship with G-D, as well as our relationship with those who are important in our lives. We set aside time regularly to spend together, to converse, and to be physically and emotionally close.

G-D gives us directions in how to have a relationship, as well as with humans, G-D's children. The first five of the Ten Commandments refer to our relationship with G-D: "I am the Lord in vain" … The second five of the Ten Commandments correlate with our relationship to our fellow humans: "Thou shall not murder, commit adultery, steal, lie, covet (desire that which belongs to, and G-D has given to, another)."

One of the key ways in which we can get closer to G-D is by reading the Torah / Old Testament / Bible, His/Her words. This book tells us what G-D expects of us, to what we must aspire, by reading about G-D's laws, and the patriarchs and matriarchs with their stellar personal character. This teaches us how to refine our own character. For example, if our enemy's animal loses its way, even several times, we are to return it over and over again. We are to take good care of our enemy's animal as if it were our own until such time as it is returned.

If both our friend and our enemy need help with their donkeys, we are to assist our enemy first, even if our friend only requires unloading and our enemy requires loading the donkey. Loading is harder than unloading. We must do what is harder for us, to help our enemy before our friend, and to help load rather than unload, in order to develop and refine our character.

We are not to bear a grudge. If our neighbors refuse to watch our children, we must not bear a grudge and refuse to watch their children when asked. We must take the higher road and watch their children. Plus, we must do so with a loving heart.

The more that we read the Torah / Old Testament / Bible, the more secrets and epiphanies G-D shares with us. We feel increasingly closer to G-D. The closeness we feel toward G-D, over time, allows our relationship with G-D to become our primary relationship. Our love for G-D translates to following those of the 613 commandments that we are able to perform today. Each commandment corresponds to a different body part. Every time we perform another commandment, a strand of light connects our particular body part to G-D. As we feel closer to G-D and perform more commandments, hundreds of strands of light are formed, connecting our different body parts to G-D. Ultimately, imagine hundreds of strands of light between our bodies and G-D. There is so much light connecting us to G-D, that we are fused with G-D, united, one with the Source.

We receive so much light and energy and love from G-D that if our spouse disappoints us or our children are struggling, we can be more understanding and compassionate. We are not so dependent on them to be a certain way. We can accept our loved ones as they are. We are receiving our primary love, closeness, and grace from G-D. G-D is our main resource. We are resourcing the Source. Therefore, we do not think we must have the people or things around us, behave in, or be a certain way for us to feel safe and happy. All can be on their own spiritual trajectories, at their own rates, and we are still okay. Again, G-D is our main sustenance.

We see ourselves and all others as inside of G-D. We are all safe, no matter which circumstances or souls magnetize. The circumstances are merely perfect conditions for our souls to learn and grow. G-D never gives us more than we can handle. The solution is already there, before the problem.

In Kabbalah, everything is for the best. Even the "evil" is there for us to build and refine our character, so we can strengthen our inner resolve to resist temptation. Everything is extremely well thought-out and planned for our highest good and maximal growth. All we have to do during every challenge is to ask ourselves, "What am I to learn?" We usually must summon up strength and courage to do something that is difficult for us, that causes us to stretch beyond our comfort zones.

When we master something that seemed completely out of our reach, ultimately we are exhilarated, uplifted, and empowered. This is accessing the G-Dly part of ourselves, where anything and everything is possible.

When we shrink from the lesson (possibly avoiding it out of fear), we think we have dodged that bullet and the war is over. This could not be further from the truth. We can never avoid our lessons permanently. G-D simply gives us a retake, but now the stakes are higher. If we attempt to avoid again, that same lesson will likely be thrown at us with even worse negative consequences. For example, if repeatedly, you do not face taking better care of yourself because you are so busy taking care of others, this lesson may develop into a severe, life-or-death illness, where you must take care of yourself or die.

When we do amass the strength and courage to overcome our greatest obstacles, we have found the G-D within. We have ascended.

This earthly life is a series of opportunities to ascend. The more we avoid, the more we struggle, the harder the opportunities become. Since the lessons never go away, the wise ones face and work on the lessons early on, before the negative consequences may be irreversible.

When we realize that this is what each of us is involved in throughout this earthly journey, we can have compassion for one another. We can feel empathy. We can give grace and forgiveness. We can perceive how we are all one, all inside of G-D, with G-D inside of us. We no longer feel separate—from G-D, from our spouses, from our children, our parents, friends, neighbors, communities. We no longer feel apart from children being raped or tortured, even if they are geographically on the other side of the world. In truth, we are inside of them, and they are inside of us.

If we take the bodies out of the picture for a moment, all that is left is energy. All energy is touching and intermingling with all other energy. We are all a part of the vast energy. What we do, think, and say affects all the other energy. When we treat ourselves and each other lovingly, it permeates and impacts the entire energy field. We all ascend together. The Messiah arrives. Peace on earth. Swords are beaten into plowshares; illnesses are cured.

Or if we choose to treat each other insensitively and cruelly, we all go down together.

Let us choose to treat this diffuse, omnipresent, omniscient energy with the utmost of reverence, caring, love, and concern, as we would our own individuated, beloved children. I am certain that is how G-D would want us to behave toward all of His/Her children and creatures—to be nonjudgmental, to be tolerant, to respect each other's differences, to talk to each other, to work things out, and to hand down a majestic, loving earth for all of our descendants, all of G-D's children, grandchildren, and great-grandchildren to inherit and enjoy!

# *Lutheran*

The Lutheran Church is named after Martin Luther, who spoke against the Roman Catholic Church. His belief is that "individual conscience is responsible to God alone"[13] and the church does not have the right to dictate how faith is used. Luther's followers were nicknamed Lutheran, and these protesters became known as Protestants. By the 1870s the Lutheran Church became the fourth largest Protestant group in America. "The Lutheran Churches base their faith on the three general creeds of Christendom: Nicene, one God; Athenian, rules of faith and Apostles."[14] A brief summary of the apostles' teaching is that the Bible shows the rules and standards of faith and practice. Therefore the Bible is the word of God.

## Finding a Spokesperson

I called and made an appointment with Reverend Paul Moldenhauer at the church in which he officiates. We met in his office, located within the school at the church. In our discussion I told Reverend Moldenhauer about the difficulty I was having in getting leaders from different religions to explain how they viewed God. Reverend Moldenhauer expressed surprise that others were not willing to explain their thoughts and immediately offered to help on this book. The reverend is an extremely warm and kind man, and it is

---

[13] Frank S. Mead and Samuel S. Hill, *Handbook of Denominations in the United States 11th Edition*, revised by Craig D. Atwood (Nashville: Abington Press, 2001), 204.

[14] Ibid.

apparent why he is so liked within his community. The following is Reverend Paul Moldenhauer's essay, entitled "Who Is My God? A Lutheran Christian Answer."

## By Reverend Paul Moldenhauer

To address the question "Who is my God?" it is helpful to first ask, "How can people know God?" One way anyone can know God is through nature. Just like we can learn something about an architect and builder from observing a building, anyone can know God by observing the universe designed and built by God. Whether through the complexity of the genome, the order in the solar system, or the beauty of a sunset, anyone can learn about God from nature. From this source, anyone can learn, for example, that God is powerful, extraordinarily intelligent, and orderly. Secondly, anyone can know God through their conscience. Just like a computer that has a built-in operating system, all humans are hardwired with a conscience, a moral system of accountability to God. From this source, anyone can learn that God is morally perfect and has that standard for humans. (By the way, if one accepts these natural sources of knowledge about God, then one concludes that an atheist is someone who consciously or subconsciously denies that built-in knowledge of God.)

The advantage of these two sources of God-knowledge is that they are accessible to all humans, which is evidenced by the consistently high percentage of people in every society who believe in the existence of a supreme supernatural being. It is upon this so-called natural knowledge of God that there are similarities among belief systems in, for example, moral standards. However, there are two significant disadvantages of natural knowledge of God: it doesn't tell us who God is; and, though it tells us that humans haven't lived up to God's standard, it doesn't tell us how to "make peace with God." Furthermore, humans are biased observers who can easily distort this natural knowledge of God for self-serving purposes.

Now, it is logical to assume that God would want humans to know him and know how to "make peace with him." It is also logical to assume that God would want that information to be available in a way that could be accurately passed on to people of all times and all cultures. So it is logical to assume that God would put that information in a book. That is not only logical; it is what God did. He revealed himself in a book called the Bible, which, though written by humans, was inspired by God himself to accurately communicate his ideas in the very words he desired to communicate those ideas. (As an aside, since God was the author behind the authors, the Bible has supernatural qualities, such as fulfilled prophecy, which make it a unique book.) By studying the self-revelation of God in the Bible, anyone can now get an accurate understanding who God is and how to make peace with him.

So what does God tell us about himself in the Bible? One answer would be: more than can be recounted in this short essay. Let's confine the answer to that which is especially pertinent to a book of this type. First, God tells us in the Bible that he is the one and only supreme supernatural being. Though there are other supernatural beings called angels, whom God created, he alone is God. Though there is a leading evil angel called Satan or the devil, who wars against God, his people, and his ways, God is the supreme supernatural being. God is not one of many supreme supernatural beings. Rather, he is the one and only supreme supernatural being.

Second, God tells us in the Bible that he alone has always existed and will always exist. God created matter and life. Angels and humans have a beginning and will live eternally, either in heaven or hell. But only God has always existed.

Third, God has revealed himself in the Bible to be three distinct persons (Father, Son Jesus, and Holy Spirit) in one God. Christianity coined a term for this: Trinity, three in one. It is logical to assume that a supreme being would be more complex than human minds could conceive. This is, in fact, what God has revealed about himself.

Fourth, God has revealed himself in the Bible as embodying justice and amazing grace. As an undistorted guilty conscience makes clear, all humans have come up short of God's moral standard of perfection. Because of his perfect nature, nothing imperfect can dwell in God's presence, just like darkness cannot exist in the presence of light. So God cannot be like a teacher who grades tests on a curve and lets us exist in his presence anyway. Nor can he be like an unjust judge who lets the guilty go free without punishment. That is bad news for humans because it means that all of us are separated from a relationship with God now and are hell-bound for eternity.

But there is good news that has its origin in God's amazing grace. The word *grace* means underserved kindness. Though humans don't deserve it, God loves humans so much that he came up with a way to restore our relationship with him, while yet upholding his justice. God himself came into this world, taking a human nature into the divine nature of God the Son Jesus. Jesus set aside the full and constant use of his nature to live the morally perfect life as a substitute for humans. And Jesus endured fully the just divine punishment for every shortcoming of every human ever, when he died on the cross. Then, Jesus rose from death and ascended into heaven.

The good news is that anyone who believes in Jesus freely receives the benefits of what Jesus did. This includes having our immorality replaced with Jesus's perfect moral standing; enjoying the blessings of a restored relationship with God as our Father and we as his children; having Jesus alive to lead, protect, and help us today; and being assured that just as Jesus rose from death, we too will physically rise to live with Jesus in heaven.

Thus, God is worthy of honor, worship, and a life lived for him!

# Messianic Judaism

Messianic Judaism was started by Evangelical Jews. Each church uses both the Old and New Testaments, therefore giving the church a Jewish style of religion. The primary beliefs of the religion are in the divinity of Jesus/Yeshua and that the Bible is absolute. The church also stresses that an individual can only reach salvation through Jesus/Yeshua.

## Finding a Spokesperson

I met Pastor Brickner after attending a service he officiated. He invited me to join his congregation for lunch. When the luncheon was finished, Pastor Brickner gave me his home number, so we could set up another meeting to discuss my project further. A few weeks later, I went to Congregational Leader Harold Brickner's home, where he agreed to participate in this book. He handed me a pamphlet that he wrote titled "The God of the Impossible." The following are excerpts taken from Pastor Brickner's writing.

## By Congregational Leader Harold Brickner

Adonai, the God of the *Tenach*, holy scriptures, is *exactly* what the aforementioned title says, "The God of the Impossible." At times, God will allow us to experience problems that are so difficult, only God could extricate us and deliver us!

The Ten Commandments are introduced with the following words:

> I am Adonai, the LORD, your God who brought you out of the land of Egypt, out of the house of bondage. (Exodus 20:2)

All of us are in a type of bondage when we enter this world. King David, the psalmist, describes our conditions in these words:

> Surely I have been a sinner from birth, Sinful from the time my mother conceived me. (Psalm 51:5)

In this "sinful" state, we have no intimate relationship with God, and most human beings don't give that relationship a very important priority. Consequently, we have no definitive statement concerning *why* we are here and *where we go* after we leave the body. Rabbis indicate that there *is* such a state called *olam haba*, eternal life, but they have no explanation as to how we can appropriate eternal life.

At seventeen years of age, I faced a major trial in my life when my father was diagnosed with lung cancer and was given less than a year to live. That summer my mother and father went on a vacation. While they were away, a friend of my aunt came to our house with her associate. Both women explained to us how Yeshua had fulfilled the prophecies of the *Tenach* (the Old Testament) concerning the Messiah. Prior to this experience, I viewed the New Testament as a gentile Bible and Jesus as the God of the gentiles. After their visit I suddenly obtained a voracious appetite for the scriptures. I diligently compared the prophecies of the Tenach with their fulfillment in *B'rit Chadasha* (the New Testament). The evidence seemed to point overwhelmingly to the fact that Yeshua (Jesus) is the Jewish Messiah. Because I wanted to worship the true God and not a false God, the following was the first prayer I uttered that was composed by me alone and came from my own heart: "God of Abraham, Isaac, and Jacob, show me whether or not Yeshua is really the Jewish Messiah."

The Lord started speaking to me powerfully through his word and through his spirit. I also had dreams in which Yeshua was being confirmed to me as the Messiah. Two sections of Tenach that proved to be most convincing in establishing Yeshua as the promised Messiah were Isaiah 52:13–53:12 and Micah 5:2 (5:1 in the Hebrew scriptures). In the former section of scriptures, Isaiah pictures Messiah as the suffering servant of Adonai, making atonement for the sins of humankind: "We all, like sheep have gone astray, each of us turned to his own way; and the LORD has laid on him the iniquity of us all" (Isaiah 53:6). Later, I learned that the Babylonian Talmud interprets Isaiah chapter 53 to be referring to the Messiah (Babylonian Talmud, tractate Sanhedrin, Perek Chelek, Folio 98). The later verse, Micah 5:2 (5:1 in the Hebrew scriptures) states: "But you, Bethlehem Ephrathah, though you are small among the clans of Judah, out of you will come for me one who will be ruler over Israel, whose origins are from of old, from days of eternity."

The Messiah would come from Bethlehem. He would be king over the Jewish people. Messiah's origins would be "from days of eternity" (Hebrew *"me-may o-lahm"*). Only God himself would be "from days of eternity"—*eternal*! Messiah would himself be God!

Not long after asking Yeshua (Jesus) into my heart, I was immersed in his name for the forgiveness of sins and received the gift of *Ruach Hakodesh*, God's Holy Spirit. After my high school graduation, I attended Moody Bible Institute in Chicago. Later I went into the army and prior to discharge got married.

Since I was a young child, I grappled with a severe emotional disorder, which was triggered through major disruptions in my life and resulted in abnormal fear and apprehension. This problem hampered my working environment. On December 1, 1971, I sat on the couch in my living room, trying to decide my options. I reasoned with myself: "Shall I kill myself and get this whole confusing mess over? No," I replied, "because I would then face eternity in which I would have no chance to make another, less violent, decision."

Then, as if a divine light went on inside of me, I felt impelled to exclaim, "Lord Yeshua, I accept your forgiveness!" The entire burden of guilt suddenly washed away. I felt like a new creation. The Lord delivered me into better work environments, and my life had changed.

In 1990 I was called to be a congregational leader. In retrospect, not only had God used my trying mental ordeal as surgery to remove my handicap of *fear*; he called me to serve him, his people, and to reach the *lost*, particularly, "the lost sheep of the house of Israel." Praise his wonderful name!

# Methodist

Methodist churches range from liberal to conservative in nature. The reason is that each church can choose how to interpret all doctrines and how to practice their religion. "The church preaches and teaches the doctrines of the Trinity; the natural sinfulness of humankind, its fall and the need of conversion and repentance; freedom of the will; justification by faith; sanctification and holiness; future reward and punishments; the sufficiency of the scriptures for salvation; and the enabling grace of God. Two sacraments, baptism and communion, are observed."[15]

## Finding a Spokesperson

Reverend Schoenhals and I met a number of times while he was going through a transitional time in his life. He was in the process of changing his pastorship from one church to another. I found him to be an extremely kind, caring, and understanding person. After a number of discussions, Reverend Schoenhals agreed to participate in this book. When he sent me his essay, Reverend Schoenhals thanked me for my persistence in challenging him. The following is Reverend Schoenhals's essay, titled "God: An Essay."

---

[15] Frank S. Mead and Samuel S. Hill, *Handbook of Denominations in the United States 11th Edition*, revised by Craig D. Atwood (Nashville: Abington Press, 2001), 229.

## By Reverend Robert D. Schoenhals

An old Jewish maxim says something like, "God is not nice. God is not your uncle. God is a volcano," or a hurricane, or a tsunami, or a raging fire. That is not to say that God is the divine bringer of destruction on humanity. Rather, God is a power loose in this world that can't be controlled, categorized, or completely understood by our human notions we name "God."

We humans have tried, of course. From the classic First Cause to the Unmoved Mover to Anselm's head-scratching yet oddly sensible definition, "God is that of which nothing greater can be conceived," all of our human efforts to define, explain, or understand God inevitably fall short.

Most but not all Christians think of God in terms of the Trinity — traditionally Father, Son and Holy Spirit — or in nonsexist terms, Creator, Christ, and Holy Spirit (not an exact equivalent, to be sure, but helpful images nonetheless). This one God in three persons is a paradox, which causes confusion for some and disbelief in others. It is troubling to our strictly monotheistic Jewish and Islamic sisters and brothers, even though we consider ourselves monotheistic as well. If these three persons of the Trinity, inferred from but not explicit in the Bible, are ways God has chosen to be revealed to humanity, then why only three? Are there not many ways for God to be known? Other modes for "knowing" God, Christians would say, are metaphors, images, descriptions of God-in-action, or other explanations of the divine presence, all potentially true according to our limited understanding. Yet the notion of God actually *revealed in three persons* in whatever sense we can make of it is something beyond and above human descriptions. So say Orthodox Christians.

Sadly, those "outside" such orthodoxy and even other Christians have occasionally lost their lives over such distinctions. Even within doctrinal Christianity there remains disagreement. The Western Church (predominantly Roman Catholic–based) says that the Holy Spirit proceeds from both the Father and the Son. The Eastern

Church (predominantly the Orthodox communions) says that the Holy Spirit proceeds from the Father *through* the Son. The modern response is likely to be, "Who cares?" At one time people cared a great deal—to the point of being willing to die for the distinction. One can debate the wisdom of such theological hair-splitting while respecting the passion with which the beliefs were held. I have benefited from a remark by the late Fuller Seminary ethicist, Lewis Smedes, who said, "I believe that God is Three-in-One, but if someday I find out that God is Four-in-One, it's not going to destroy my faith."

And so we struggle. It seems to me there is something innate in humanity that wants to believe in a Higher Power, not aloof but intimately related to life in our world, yet not exactly one with it either. Those who choose not to believe are making a legitimate choice based on their own perceptions, no less humanly limited than those who choose to believe. The Deists, enlightened thinkers who included most of our early American fathers of the nation, saw God as the divine clockmaker who wound everything up in the beginning and then watched it all from afar, not involved in the day-to-day affairs of nature or humanity. One can see evidence for this view, yet it seems to fall short of our yearnings for God.

For myself, two images give me both insight and comfort. I see God as the passionately devoted divine parent and as the suffering creator. Both metaphors are found scattered throughout the Bible. Neither can be entirely separated from the other. A brief explanation: By God's very nature as Creator, God loves what God has created—all of it. (I will not enter into a discussion of God's modes or methods in creation; to me eons are every bit as creative as short term.) As parent, God longs for what is best for the child—human and otherwise—at the same time knowing that the child cannot always be shielded from the consequences of foolish actions. Thus the earth suffers, and God suffers. When we destroy ourselves and each other, God suffers. The crucifixion of Jesus the Christ is God's powerful statement of the extent to which God is willing to suffer on behalf of God's people, who so often get it wrong. "Father, forgive them for they do not know what they do," is more than Jesus's simple statement of forgiveness for his executioners. It is a cosmic statement on behalf of a suffering creator or a divine parent.

Yet the Christians' belief in a resurrection, shared to varying degrees and with different understandings among several other religions, is God's way of saying, "I will not be defeated. I will have the last word." It is also God's affirmation that it is possible for humanity to get it right, to become more godlike in thought, word, and deed.

If we humans are, in fact, the offspring of God, the creations of God, then our destiny certainly has something to do with growing into a likeness of our parent or our creator. As Paul suggests, the whole of creation is groaning together, as if in the pains of childbirth, waiting for something new to be born in this world, something intimately related to our own relationship with God. The whole of creation is waiting — but not passively — for God's children to actively live that role and that destiny. All will be the beneficiaries when that happens. To say more would require another essay.

Conclusion: To those who seem bent on "proving" God or defending God or convincing others to believe all the proper things about God, I am often tempted to reply, "Where do we get our arrogance?" Let God be God. God has done quite well without each of us and our answers for quite some time now. Let God be as wild and unpredictable as the wind. Let God be free to act, not according to our limited wishes but according to God's mysterious ends. Let God be God, knowing that behind it all is a passionate love that embraces all that God has made — flawed and frail yet potential-ridden humans included.

# *Mormon*

Mormons use both the Old and New Testaments in their services. However, they base much of their beliefs on the Book of Mormon, which was discovered by Joseph Smith. They also use two other books written by Smith in their service: *Doctrine and Covenants* and *The Pearl of Great Price*. Their belief is that Joseph Smith restored the authentic church, which had gone underground for many centuries. Individuals who belong to the Mormon Church have a high degree of loyalty and dedication to the church. Most Mormons are conservative, morally and politically. Family involvement in the church is highly valued in the Mormon faith.

## Finding a Spokesperson

The Mormons, at the beginning, hampered any form of interaction. My first three attempts to set up a meeting were rebuffed. In a conversation with retired barrister Ed Cherkinsky, he stated that he interfaced with some individuals of the Mormon faith in a volunteer group, and he would ask one if they would help me. He then gave me a phone number, and I contacted that individual. She gave me the phone number to her bishop. I met with Bishop Jensen at his office in a Church of Jesus Christ of Latter-Day Saints. He is an extremely nice man who said he would help me with this book, as long as I received permission from the person in authority above him. I contacted that individual, and after a few discussions, he gave Bishop Jensen permission to write about his perception of God. The following is the essay that Bishop Jensen wrote.

## By Bishop Trescott E. Jensen

As a member of the Church of Jesus Christ of Latter-Day Saints, I submit this statement for myself, not in any official capacity for the church. I accept full responsibility for the content of this declaration of my testimony, knowledge, and experience. — Terscott E. Jensen

When I was a child, I learned "The Articles of Faith of The Church of Jesus Christ of Latter-Day Saints." These thirteen statements summarized the basic doctrine of the church. The first four are relevant to the subject of this essay, my concept and understanding of God. They are:

1. We believe in God, the Eternal Father, and His Son, Jesus Christ, and in the Holy Ghost.
2. We believe that men will be punished for their own sins, and not for Adam's transgressions.
3. We believe that through the atonement of Christ, all humankind will be saved by obedience to the laws and ordinances of the Gospel.
4. We believe that the first principles and ordinances of the Gospel are: first, faith in the Lord Jesus Christ; second, Repentance; third, Baptism by immersion for the remission of sins; fourth, laying on of hands for the gift on the Holy Ghost.

This is the root and core of my personal understanding of God, where I came from, why I am here, and where I am going. Joseph Smith, a prophet, saw God the Father and His Son, Jesus Christ, and testified to the world they were separate individuals and as tangible as man.

As a young man, I served a two-year mission in Scotland as a representative of the church. During that time of service, study, and prayer, I gained my own witness of the nature of my heavenly Father, Jesus Christ, and the Holy Ghost. The reality of God, the eternal Father, is clear to me. He has tangible physical characteristics, and we are in his image. Jesus Christ, his eldest spirit child, declared that he is like his Father, our Father in heaven. Therefore, those who see Christ have seen the Father. The Holy Ghost is a personage of spirit and makes himself manifest as a witness of good and truth and encourages all men on earth to become their best. These three individuals are distinct members of what is referred to as the Godhead. They are unified in three specific goals for us, the spirit children of God the eternal Father. They are (1) to provide an opportunity for the spirit children of the Father to gain a body, (2) to learn the principle of agency (to choose good or evil), and (3) to provide a means whereby those who have lived on earth may return into the presence of God the Father.

Our Father in heaven presides and directs the affairs of this earth. Jesus Christ accepted his role as Savior and Redeemer while a spirit child of our heavenly Father, before this earth was created. He was born on this earth and gained a physical body. The Savior was resurrected following his death, as prophesied and recorded in scripture. Jesus Christ has always been and continues to be our advocate with the Father. The Holy Ghost provides, to those who exercise a particle of faith and who seek truth, a witness — we are not alone.

Two key characteristics of God are truth and love. Our Father in heaven, Jesus Christ, and the Holy Ghost are the source of all truth. They are also examples of pure love. I know that God loves me. He knows me, and I have learned that following the example of Jesus Christ brings happiness into my life. Looking beyond ourselves and being in the service of others is a reliable source of joy. Family relationships, knowledge, and our experiences are all we take with us after this life. To that end, it is expedient we utilize every opportunity to enrich family interaction, be continually learning and anxiously engaged in good works.

I am grateful for this opportunity to express my understanding of where I came from, why I am here, and where I am going. As spirit children of our Father in heaven, we share a divine heritage. It is a blessing to know that Jesus Christ is my brother, a child of God. I have experienced the influence of the Holy Ghost in my life and in the lives of others. One day, we will all be resurrected and become physically and eternally in the image of God. We will stand before God our Father and report on our use of agency. We will join with our family and thank God for his love. It will be glorious when the need for opposition has passed and the demands of justice are met by the atonement of Christ. It is my prayer that all men will come to know we are children of God and that he loves us.

# Native American

Christianity in different forms is the largest religion for Native Americans. However, traditional beliefs have been exercised through oral interpretation in Native American communities. "The book *Black Elk Speaks* has been a guide for whites and natives alike who are seeking to connect with a nature-based mysticism in which 'Mother Earth' and all her inhabitants live in ecological and spiritual harmony. Shamanism, sweat lodges, vision quests, and other feathers of some tribal religions have become part of the American religious economy."[16]

## An Interview with Jerry Celend

I was introduced to Jerry Celend in one of those strange circumstances that have been happening since I started this book. My wife and I went out with a group of friends for dinner. At the restaurant, one of the group invited friends of theirs to join us. By happenstance I sat next to the couple, and in our discussion I talked about working on this book. They mentioned that they knew a Native American who may be interested in sharing his thoughts for this book. A few days later, I was given Jerry Celend's phone number. I called Jerry, and it took a few months to set up a couple of meetings. Jerry is an extremely sincere person, and once you start talking to him, you feel as if you have known him for years. He was an activist in his community, has been written up in the

---

[16] Frank S. Mead and Samuel S. Hill, *Handbook of Denominations in the United States 11th Edition*, revised by Craig D. Atwood (Nashville: Abington Press, 2001), 242.

news, and has appeared on local television to share his views on how Native Americans view religion. Jerry has also presented at a number of interfaith meetings. The following is an excerpt from our conversation about "Who is God?"

Native Americans have always tried to live in concert, in harmony, with all that is around them in this turtle island we call North America. We only have one God, whom we call Gitche Manitou, the creator of the universe. The term *Gitche Manitou* means the Great Spirit. If you want to look at how great this spirit is, you only have to study a flower, how small and complex this entity appears.

Gitche Manitou is like a father figure to us. He can do things we cannot conceive of as a native people. We thank him in the songs we sing. We thank him for this life we have and for the good health we have. We thank the Great Spirit for being able to see and hear and do all sorts of other things. He allows us to do good things in life and always be positive about life.

The old teachings keep us attuned to meet the challenges of today. These teachings will not let you down. They are moral teachings. They do not teach you to drink alcohol or take drugs. Many young people today have the attitude that they can do whatever they wish. What it is all about is helping people. Because man's life is very short, the time on the mountain is very long. We are only going to be here for a short amount of years. It is important that people remember us in a good light, not to impress, but to be who we are. People will respect that. I have traveled a great deal and found that to be true. What you do now in this lifetime is very important, not just for you but for your children and grandchildren. In our story of the wolf, which we pass from generation to generation, we have learned that we harmonize with one another and that we respect the land.

I'm from the Ojibwa tribe. We are located in the Upper Peninsula of Michigan. The Ojibwas were all across Canada, Wisconsin, Michigan, and Minnesota. In Montana the Ojibwa are called Chippewa. We meet twice a year, once in the spring and once in the fall. We open our sweat lodge in the spring to get the spiritual side going and close the lodge in the fall because winter is coming. We have a lot of ceremonies. The ceremonies are for all the things the Good Lord has given to us. We also have our spiritual helpers, the manitous; they are like angels. They look after us and help us out, and they also look after the earth. God has touched every nation with a message. The messages are not the same but different. When the nations get together, conflict comes in, because of the different messages. We cannot afford the luxury of conflict. Now is the time when we really must dig down and turn around the problems we have.

# Orthodox Christianity

The Orthodox Church is made up of a number of churches from different countries. Each church service "reflects its own national heritage and ethnic customs in its liturgy."[17] There is no single hierarchy for the different Orthodox churches. The hierarchy is based on the country of origin. However, there is a common thread that runs throughout all Orthodox churches. The church structure, movements by the priests, and words spoken by the congregation have symbolic value. "Orthodox Christians hold that since God became incarnate in Christ, God's human nature may be depicted in sacred image."[18] Therefore, sanctified icons of figures and events are central to the Orthodox religion. However, these pictures may not be three-dimensional. The Nicene Creed is central to all Orthodox churches. The churches believe in baptism, penance, holy orders, confirmation, Eucharist (communion), and extreme unction (last rites). They do not believe in purgatory; however they do offer prayers for the dead, because the church believes the dead pray for people on earth.

## Finding a Spokesperson

I was introduced to Father George through an e-mail sent by Steve Spreitzer, CEO of the Michigan Roundtable for Diversity and Inclusion. Father George and I interacted by e-mail a few times.

---

[17] Frank S. Mead and Samuel S. Hill, *Handbook of Denominations in the United States 11th Edition*, revised by Craig D. Atwood (Nashville: Abington Press, 2001),243.

[18] Mead and Hill, 246.

He was gracious enough to allow me to interview him a couple of times. I found his background amazing and what he went through to practice his religion fascinating. The office in which we met was covered with pictures of his parishioners and letters of thanks and accolades on all walls. It was obvious how he felt about his flock and how his parishioners felt about him.

## By Father George Shalhoub

The question of who is God to me came from the teachings of my family. We went to church twice a week and on religious holidays. We learned how God had relationships with people. For non-Christians, God sometimes seems to be invisible, but for us who are called Orthodox Christians, the incarnation is the main source of understanding who God is. For us God takes on human flesh, not because he cannot be wondrous, magical, awesome, and miraculous in so many ways, but to allow men and women to reflect on the attributes of God. God to me always comes in the faces I see. Because in those faces we behold Christ, we behold God, born of the Virgin Mary; he lived, cried, was circumcised, baptized, ate, and got hungry. If anyone can't relate to a person who lived like Christ, they could never understand God.

The tragedy is sometimes people make up in their own mind an image of their own God, and the God they imagine may be an answer to their own political or economic surroundings. Many people feel that when they use the word *God*, it becomes very powerful and exonerates their actions. That is why you find people killed in the name of God. People are abused in the name of God and judged in the name of God. To me God comes in prayer, God comes in ritual, God comes in a most reflective and personal way. John Zizioulas stated, "a person cannot be imagined in himself but only in his relationships and in the ecclesiastical context, personhood is realized solely through freedom in love." I agree with those statements.

In the Eucharist, when I stand at the altar and say, "On behalf of Christ, eat; this is his body, and drink; this is his blood," in reality it makes the entire community a member of one body. But that is not enough if we do not reflect this membership in actions. Therefore, God to me is in the faces of all who walk on this earth, even if they do not subscribe to my religion.

Whether God chose me or I chose God to be an Orthodox Christian, I reflect that God can love a little bit more, can forgive a little bit more, can be less hostile a little bit more, and can be welcoming a little bit more. In reading from the book of Psalms and the New Testament, we see in God Christ, who spoke for the poor, who defended minorities, and who despised prejudice and racism. There are so many examples of that in all of his teachings. His teachings remind men and women why they are created, so that they can reflect God to others. Now in my own religion, it is done in the midst of silence and in the midst of chaos, in the midst of meditation and dance. We are made in the image and likeness of God, in the divine image.

When I visit a hospital and pray with someone who is dying, I sometimes break down. I am then comforted by the sick person. This makes me realize that God is there and is waiting for me to come home. All that I have said can be described in holy books. How we live, the way we were born, and how we die.

I think that today, understanding of who God is to me forces me to realize that I no longer live in only an Orthodox Christian world. I think that other religions are beginning to understand that they no longer live in a secular world and that they need to reach out to others. America can be the greatest test of explaining who God is to others. Because in America—thank God for that—no religion can regulate who you are and what you can and cannot do. The issue of separation of church and state has forced many religions in the world to coexist with others. The understanding of the basic principles of democracy was really brought up by religion, by the church, by Christ who said the least count and those who cannot vote count.

There is a beautiful passage out of the Gospel of St. John that is read on Easter. It states, "In the beginning there was the word and the word was God" (John 1:1). Those who accept him are called the children of God. God never forces you to follow him; it is always an invitation and sometimes a costly one. There is also a reading that was written in the third century about who God calls on Easter night. He calls those who have fasted for forty days and those who have not, those who came early and those who came late, because at the end we all matter.

In my own life, I learned about the virtues of God. I asked myself what God would ask me to do. I don't have to accept everything. I don't have to accept another's way of life; that is their life. I don't have to accept another's way of dress; that is their dress. I don't expect others to impose their religious rules on me. God transcends human boundaries if we allow him. God transcends universal obstacles if we allow him. Many people think that the ritual or rubric is a problem with religion, but it is not. You are really becoming more enriched by following the rituals and rubrics.

I learned about religion in Syria. My family, who are Orthodox Christians, were a minority. We lived in Hama, which is all Sunni (Muslim) and is considered to be a Mecca outside of Mecca. People, who are very religious, very good and kind, live in separate neighborhoods. We were all cordial to one another and knew each other's history. My family was not privileged enough to go to private school to learn about our faith; we went to public school. One day my brother and I came home early from school because the teacher allowed us to leave when Islam was being taught, and we were Christians. My father was really offended that we came home early, and he said, "You are to go back to class." I asked why, and he stated, "In order to live in this world, you have to understand what others believe. You don't live alone; you live with others."

We went back to school, and I ended up receiving a certificate for how well I excelled in Muslim religious class. When I went to the seminary, the ritual, the worship of the sacrament, and the movement in the pictures reminded me of what God has done for us, that he loves us; that he cares for all people. When I look at the pictures of people in my office, I see God in the faces of each and every one of them. I pray for them and offer them to God, and God in return offers them to me, to take care of them.

# Orthodox Judaism

Orthodox Judaism believes that the Torah (the first five books of the Bible) should be followed as written. They also believe that the *Halakah* (the set of rules and practices for daily living) are not subject to change. The Orthodox Union in America was founded by Rabbi Henry Mendes in 1898. Its purpose is to oversee that both the Torah and Halakah are being followed. In Orthodox Judaism, intermarriage and assimilation are seen as threats to the survival of Judaism.

## An Interview with Rabbi Elimelech Silverberg

While in a Home Depot, I saw a gentleman who looked like a rabbi. I walked up to him and introduced myself. He stated his name was Rabbi Weinberg. I explained to him that I was working on a book about "Who is God?" and asked him if he knew of anyone who may be interested in participating. Rabbi Weinberg immediately said that there was one man who was a true scholar and had written about the Jewish religion. That man was Rabbi Silverberg. I called Rabbi Silverberg, and he was kind enough to meet with me three times. The last time we met, we sat in the library of his synagogue, and this interview took place.

(In Orthodox Judaism, you do not write the word *God*. Therefore, a hyphen replaces the *o*.)

Judaism is based on the teachings of the Torah. The Torah contains and includes what is called the twenty-four books of the scriptures. That's called the written tradition. There is also the oral tradition, which we believe comes from G-d. I believe Moses was the lawgiver. When he went up to Sinai to receive the Torah, he was taught by G-d both the scriptures and the oral tradition that explains the scriptures. The Torah contains ideas of Jewish law and ideas of theology. If we look into the Torah and the five books of Moses, we find that G-d has no shape, has no form, and has no image.

One of the most important statements in the five books of Moses is "Hear, O Israel; the Lord is our G-d, the Lord is one!" According to the oral tradition, what this means is that this oneness of G-d, the essence of G-d, pervades everything. Therefore, everything is included in what we call the G-dhead. The Jewish understanding is that what we say in our prayers is that G-d recreates the world in perpetuity. So existence in the world as we know it emerges in perpetuity from nothing to something.

According to the oral tradition, G-d deliberately creates the world in a sense of independence from G-d, in a sense of separation from G-d. But the reality is that nothing is separated from G-d. Divine energy that sustains life is all-pervasive; it exists in everything, whether it be inanimate or animate, vegetative or human, whether it be the woodenness of the tree or all forms of metallurgy or the DNA of human beings. All of these different aspects of life are pervaded with a divine energy that sustains these aspects of life and perpetuates these aspects of life.

The Jewish tradition teaches us that our job as G-d's chosen people is to spread the knowledge of G-d in the world. To spread this recognition that there is a G-d who sustains the world and who should be served is our mission in life as Jews. We talk about Jews being the light of the world, spreading the light of G-d even though it's inherently the world of darkness, because G-d created the world in a way that the world seems to be separated from G-d.

The mission of the Jewish people is to teach humanity that G-d is all-pervasive and must be served. He is served by following the commandments. There are commandments that show humanity, kindness, and prohibitions against homosexuality, murder, kidnapping, idolatry, and stealing. Those are essential to all of humankind. The obligation of respecting parents and giving charity is universal. Then on top of that, we as Jews have been given added commandments from the Torah that allow us to access G-d. According to our tradition, we believe that through the observance of ritual commandments, we as Jews have the opportunity to access G-d in a unique and very intimate way.

We believe that other religions who accept the unity of G-d are worthy religions. We also believe in the hereafter. It is our belief that when a person passes on, his soul enters a different dimension of time and space. We don't believe that a person has to be Jewish to enter the hereafter. Any person who follows the basic concepts of morality as described in the commandments will be granted their share in the world to come.

Our statement, "Hear, O Israel; the Lord is our G-d, the Lord is one!" doesn't just mean that there is one G-d. It means that the oneness of G-d's essence, which is called oneness, exists within everything. It is the job of man to deal with the physical things in life in a moral and ethical way, and by doing that, we are accepting the royal kingship of G-d Almighty, which is the job not of just the Jewish people but of all humankind.

# Pentecostal

There are a number of variations of the Pentecostal Church. The church "developed out of the older Holiness Churches, which in turn had come out of the Methodist Churches, which had themselves originated in the Anglican Church."[19] The Pentecostal Church, Adventist Church, and Jehovah's Witnesses all base their concept on the "idea of remaking the church according to one's understanding of the Scriptures."[20] Some of the Pentecostal churches believe in one or more of the following: prophecy, visions, healing, the gift and interpretations of tongues, original sin, truth in scriptures, future rewards and punishments, divine inspiration, and answers to prayers. Most groups follow two sacraments: Baptism and the Lord's Supper.

## Finding a Spokesperson

I met the chief apostle, Dr. Prince A. Miles, by calling his church a number of times. After I obtained an appointment with him, he offered to help me with this book. We met a few more times, and Dr. Miles gave me his background. He also gave me a sermon that he did on his radio program about God. Dr. Miles has written his own book, about the loss of his child, titled *He Was Our Prince: Faith Tested, Tried and Testified*. He has also met dignitaries and

---

[19] Frank S. Mead and Samuel S. Hill, *Handbook of Denominations in the United States 11th Edition*, revised by Craig D. Atwood (Nashville: Abington Press, 2001), 21.

[20] Ibid.

given sermons all over the world about his faith. The following are excerpts from the sermon that I received.


## By Dr. Prince A. Miles

It is important that we understand and know who God is. We all have heard about God. People want to know: Who is God? What is God? Where did God come from? Can I see God? How did God get here? We have a lot of questions about God. When we study about God, it's called theology. It's a term used in biblical proportions about the study of God, knowing God. We say all the time, "God is good." We know God is good. We know there is a God. Amen.

All of your questions can be answered in the holy Torah or the Bible. The holy Bible has the anointed word of God. All answers to all of your questions are in the holy sacred scriptures of the Bible. Bible means "collection of books." Every answer to all of your questions is in the holy scriptures, the Torah and the Bible.

The Bible is the word of God. Read your Bible so that you do not sin against God. If you don't open up your sacred scriptures, how do you know what is in it? It's not just a book; it is the word of God. It is a contract from God to man. There is nothing new today that God has not addressed in his holy word. Open up your Bible; he knows about you. Because he made you, he has created you; he designed you in his image.

God has given every man a measure of faith. If you believe in Genesis, you will be okay. It states, "In the beginning was God." In the end, as your mind can conceive it, there is God. In the middle, wherever you are, there is God. Before the beginning of what our minds can conceive and think, God was here. He is big, giant, magnificent, super-whatever adjective you can describe, he is that plus more.

We have to study the word of God so we will know what God is and what his purpose is and what his place is in your life. Jesus has a plan for my life. You need someone to share the awesome plan of your life. You are here for a divine purpose. God has us here because God has a plan, but you don't know the plan. God wants you to have dominion over everything in your life. God wants you to be victorious.

God is eternal, everlasting; God is never-ending. All things are made by God. Everything—your glasses, your tie, your shoes, socks, the table, the lights, the carpet that you walk on—everything was made by him and him alone. When you have his word within you, you have his authority. The power of God dwells within us. Verse 4, first chapter of John: "In him was life, life was meaning. He came to give you life abundantly."

Man would be most miserable if God had not made himself known. God is the author of life and salvation. The first time the Father gave him a name. His name is Jesus. He will save his people from their sins. I am talking about the name of God, Adonai. In the scriptures is the infallible name of God. God needs to be first in your life, your plate, and your agenda. When you invoke his presence, his name, he will be there. The God that I am preaching about wants you to walk in an upward way, a righteous way, to find that path and walk therein.

In the New Testament, Jesus is identified as the only Son of the Father. Many try to go around him. It's sad if Christians believe that they can go around the word of God. Jesus is the only way to salvation. Oh Lord, I am preaching about God today. He revealed himself, 1 John, verse 14: "the word was made flesh and dwelt among us and we beheld his glory, full of grace and truth." Children, sons and daughters in the gospel, wherever I go, I let them know that Jesus Christ is the answer. Amen.

# Protestant

All Protestant churches trace their roots to Martin Luther, when he broke away from the Roman Catholic Church. "Most early protestant figures saw themselves as trying to correct problems within the Roman Catholic Church. Today there are hundreds of different denominations that originally derived from the reformation movement."[21] A few of these groups are Baptist, Methodist, Presbyterian, Anglican, Episcopal, Evangelical, and Pentecostal. "Protestants counted together as a group are in fact the second largest Christian body in the world."[22] The basic beliefs that came out of the Reformation movement are called the five Solas: "by grace alone, by faith alone, by scripture alone, by Christ alone and Glory of God alone."[23] The majority of Protestant churches believe in the Nicene Creed, and "Protestantism holds that ultimate and final Authority resides solely in the Holy Scriptures."[24]

## Finding a Spokesperson

I was given Reverend Melrose's number by retired barrister Edward Cherkinsky. They both served on the board of a community nonprofit organization. Reverend Melrose and I met in the office of a church. I explained what I was trying to do, and he offered to help me by writing a short statement about his perceptions of God. He

---

[21] Protestant-Reformation; religion sprung from Catholicism, www.religious-beliefs.com/protestant-religion.htm.

[22] Protestant-The Prayer Foundation, www.prayerfoundation.org/protestant_beliefs.com.

[23] Protestant-Reformation; religion sprung from Catholicism.

[24] Protestant-The Prayer Foundation.

also gave me Steve Spreitzer's telephone number and stated that he may be able to help me on my quest. Steve Spreitzer is the CEO of the Michigan Roundtable for Diversity and Inclusion. Steve was extremely helpful; he introduced me to a number of religious leaders. The following is Reverend Paul Melrose's statement.

## By Reverend Paul J. Melrose

I am a Christian/Protestant, United Methodist Minister, retired after thirty-nine and a half years of active ministry, mostly as a pastoral counselor and licensed clinician, with some time spent in the parish as well. I understand God in pretty traditional biblical/ theological ways. God is the creator of all there is, all of life. God sustains life, and God redeems all that is. We can go on. This relates to the Christian doctrine of the Trinity, though I don't often get into too much of a detailed discussion on this. While the Christian, in my opinion, believes in the God of Abraham Isaac, Jacob, and Sarah as also the father of the Lord Jesus Christ, there is throughout both old (Hebrew) and new (Christian) scriptures an awareness of others and many hints to be hospitable and welcome the stranger. To me this suggests that though we believe and practice and see our faith as applicable and open to all, we also understand the existence of people of other faiths. While we try to be open about our faith, we need to respect them and theirs.

Two Hebrew scriptures, captured in Christian scriptures, hold up the nature of God as a God of love. Roughly translated, it is the words "Love the Lord God with all of your heart and soul and mind and strength and your neighbor as yourself." Here we summarized the nature of God and its meaning for all of God's people.

# Reform Judaism

Reform Judaism promotes assimilation into American culture for the pursuit of justice and peace. It came from the Haskalah movement in Europe. The Haskalah movement believed that in order to stop persecution, Jews should fully assimilate into the culture around them. In the 1740s Rabbi Moses Mendelsohn, following the ideas used in the Haskalah movement, endorsed the idea of assimilation by urging his followers to learn the language around them, instead of speaking Hebrew and Yiddish. This idea was brought to America in the 1840s by Rabbi Isaac Wise. The Torah in Reform Judaism is seen as terms of ethical demands, not ceremony.

## Finding a Spokesperson

Rabbi Michael Moskowitz was one of the first religious leaders I interacted with. We met at the temple in which he officiates. After some discussion, Rabbi Moskowitz agreed to participate in this book and offered to write a statement. At the time of our meeting, Rabbi Moskowitz stated that he would "get to it" and that I should continuously remind him because of time restraints. (At that time I did not realize that message would be conveyed by many other religious leaders, and the amount of time it would take to get leaders who agreed to participate in this book to follow through.) I dropped by the temple many times over a number of months. What I learned from this opportunity was how a religious organization works. The individuals who work in the office toil extremely hard to meet the demands of their organization. They take care of the paperwork, answer questions from the congregation, and set up meetings with individuals and groups. All of this helps the temple run smoothly. I also learned more about the role religious leaders have in their organization. In Rabbi Moskowitz's case (and many other religious leaders), he has many meetings that deal with birth, marriage, death, and the general running of the temple. The following is Rabbi Michael Moskowitz's statement titled "Listening for God."

## By Rabbi Michael L. Moskowitz

This is what I believe. As a liberal Jew, as a rabbi, through my studies, but even more through experience, when asked about my understanding of God, of how I see God in our world, this is what I believe. Life affords us the opportunity, the blessing to be able to listen, and in so doing, we hear what the mystics have called the still, small voice in our world.

It reminds me of the first time we learned of those words in the Bible, heard at this moment by the prophet Elijah. "There was a great and mighty wind, splitting the mountains and shattering the rocks ... But the Lord was not in the wind. After the wind, there was an earthquake; but the Lord was not in the earthquake. After the earthquake, there was a fire; but again, the Lord was not in the fire. And after the fire, a still small voice" (1 Kings 19:11–12).

It is natural for us to see God in the majestic and the grand. We stand on the top of a mountain or at the edge of the ocean or watch a magnificent sunset, and we sense the divine in our world. But what we seem to forget is where God is every day—in the quiet, the ordinary, the unexpected; the conversation, the connecting, the love. God is found in what we attune ourselves to hear.

In the relationships we treasure most, with a spouse, in what is shared and how we connect; with friends who know how to be there for us and us for them. In our community, in how we support one another and celebrate life together; we can never take these for granted. Every day, each encounter even, gives us the chance to connect, to help, to understand. In so doing, we find God in our world.

# Roman Catholic

The largest single religious group in the United States is the Roman Catholics. The church "accepts the Apostles' Creed, the Nicene-Constantinople Creed, the Athanasian Creed, and the Creed of Pius IV, also called the Creedal Statement of the Council of Trent. These creeds set forth many doctrines common to most Christian bodies, such as the Trinity (Father, Son, and Spirit are fully and completely divine without losing their distinctiveness) and full humanity and divinity of Christ."[25] The church believes that "the sacraments are a visible means receiving God's grace and are thus holy."[26] There are seven sacraments used in the Roman Catholic Church: Baptism, given to both children and adults to become members of the church; Confirmation; Eucharist (communion); Penance; Anointing; "the sacraments of holy orders is for the ordination of deacons, priests, and bishops."[27] Marriage cannot be dissolved but can be annulled. Mary, mother of Christ, is important in the church because of the belief that through prayers to Mary, she will intervene with Christ.

## Finding a Spokesperson

When first starting this project, I mentioned it to a friend named Ray Sypniewski. Ray stated that he would call his priest and try to set up an appointment for me. The three of us met a couple of

---

[25] Frank S. Mead and Samuel S. Hill, *Handbook of Denominations in the United States 11th Edition*, revised by Craig D. Atwood (Nashville: Abington Press, 2001), 95.
[26] Ibid.
[27] Mead and Hill, 96.

weeks later in the rectory of the church. We sat at an antique dining table, and I explained to Father Treppa and Ray that I was writing a book about the way people view God. Father Treppa offered to help me in my quest. The following is a letter that Father Treppa sent to me, stating his point of view.

## By Reverend Terrence F. Treppa, PhD

The more I think about your project, the more it becomes, for me, a frustration. I've met other folks who had an idea to get something across to people. Like you, they thought that all they had to do was to put it in a book, and everyone would real all about their idea, and presto, all would be solved. That these ideas are simply the best and should change people just in the reading. It doesn't happen that way.

Religion begins with an experience. A person has to be invited, brought, etc. to a religion. Joining a religion is another question. Knowing the tenets of a religion is further down the line. Finally, beginning the spiritual quest happens for a very few. Many today say they are interested in spirituality, but they are only kidding themselves. The spiritual journey is fraught with traps, dangers, delusions, setbacks, and dangers to one's soul. To undertake it on one's own is a folly.

As far as religions' teaching about God is concerned, each religion has a particular creed that it is supposed to follow. The Catholic Church has the Apostles' Creed and the Nicene Creed as the basic formulations of its tenets. We quip that the difference between a homily and sermon is that a homily is a talk on what Jesus said. A sermon is a talk on what he meant or should have said and quite often is a "hobby horse" of the preacher.

Religions are further complicated the further they get from the founder. The Catholic Church today is two thousand years removed from Jesus Christ. Even the scripture scholars have a hard time determining the "very words of Christ," let alone what he actually meant. All we have is the four gospels, and they are written from a particular point of view, addressing a specific audience. We are not the people the authors had in mind. Thus, we have what Jesus said and meant, what the followers heard and thought what he meant, and eventually what was written. Quite a bit removed from the original teaching. All we hope is that the essential teaching makes it through the filters of time, cultures, languages, and consciousness of the followers.

What some today are trying to do is to validate the teachings through scientific means. All of the literary tests have been or are being applied to the scriptures. Accurate translations are an ongoing process, simply because our culture is in flux. Some are using more advanced techniques such as muscle testing to validate the teachings of Jesus and all of the scriptures. Jesus's teachings come out as very high in integrity and authenticity.

We are still left with the reality that people have been and continue to walk away from religion. For those of us inside the Catholic religion, our hands are tied in the sense that we must conform to the liturgical norms set down by the Catholic Church. We can form study groups, prayer groups, small groups, basic communities, etc. to give our fellow parishioners an experience with religion that hopefully will lead them to begin the spiritual journey. Quietly within the Catholic Church, and I believe within all religions, there is a gradual transformation that is happening. Only time will tell.

# Seventh-Day Adventist

The Seventh-Day Adventist is the largest of the Adventist churches. The Adventist movement started with the same thoughts as Pentecostals and Jehovah's Witnesses, that scripture can be remade based on one's understanding. The churches named Seventh-Day Adventist came about because they believe that the Sabbath should be on the seventh day and that "the observation of the Sabbath was to be a way to await the Advent of the Lord."[28] They believe in the gift of prophecy and follow the prophecies of Ellen White in the doctrine and structure of the church. The Seventh-Day Adventists believe that the Bible holds the "authoritative nature of revelation of God."[29] Some of their distinctive practices include foot washing to prepare for communion, immersion of adults for baptism, and using the Sabbath as a day to rest and worship. The church promotes separation of church and state and believes in religious liberty.

## Finding a Spokesperson

I came into contact with the Seventh-Day Adventists through a phone call. It was answered by an extremely nice woman who was in charge of the food bank for the church. We talked a few times; she then invited me to hear the interim pastor of her church. That pastor was Reverend Cottrell. The first time we met, he did not

---

[28] Frank S. Mead and Samuel S. Hill, *Handbook of Denominations in the United States 11th Edition*, revised by Craig D Atwood (Nashville: Abington Press, 2001), 35.

[29] Mead and Hill, 36.

have time to sit down with me. The second time was after a service at the church. Reverend Cottrell is an extremely warm man who likes to give unscripted services. He gave me a copy of his sermon to use for this book. The following are excerpts from his sermon.

## By Reverend Stanley Cottrell

How do we stay focused on Jesus? You read this book every day. Not just on Sabbath morning. An hour on Sabbath morning or three hours on Sabbath morning is not going to do it for you. You can't come to church and go home and live like the devil. Well, let me rephrase that. You can't come to church and live like a Christian, then go home and live like the devil. We are Christians seven days a week. You cannot change and put it on for Sabbath morning, then put if off the rest of the week. You need to feed on God's word. Ellen White says in *Great Controversy,* "Only those who have fortified their minds with words of truth in the Bible will stand in the final conflict." Do you want to be an overcomer? Do you want to have words to speak when they call you before the councils and the courts? Those words can be brought to your mind only if they have been there beforehand. Read and pray. When we let Jesus into our hearts, we're opening the door to him. We are saying to him, "Come on in, take control of my life; I want to get to know you." We know him by studying his book and praying. We get to know Jesus, and to know him is to love him; to let the love of Christ constrain us and compel us, to give us the strength and power to move upward.

Jesus, it's all about Jesus. Jesus is the same yesterday, today, and forever. He promises that he'll be with us always—even unto the end of time. Do you believe that? Do we claim it? There is a text in 1 Thessalonians 5:16: "Rejoice always, pray without ceasing. In everything give thanks: for this is the will of Christ Jesus for you. Do not quench the spirit. Do not despise prophecies, test all things; hold fast that which is good. Abstain from every form of evil." Is that good advice? You know about this little book? It's called *Steps to Christ,* thirteen chapters. I've often said a chapter a day will keep the evil away. This is on page 61: "As we meditate upon the perfections of the savior, we shall desire to be holy, transformed, and renewed in the image of his purity. There will be a hungering and thirsting of soul to become like him, who we adore. The more our thoughts are upon Christ, the more we shall speak of him to others, and represent him to the world." Who are your thoughts on? Are they on Jesus, or are they on the world? We do not know what we shall be. But when he shall appear, we shall be like him, for we shall see him as he is; because we have kept our eyes on Jesus.

Heavenly Father, help us to let Jesus into our hearts, to let him control our lives, to control our thoughts, to control our words. Help us to be ready when he comes, because we have pressed on. We have stayed focused on Jesus. We have overcome through the power that Jesus gives us, and we want to sit with him on his throne.

# Shia Muslim/Islam

Shi'ites are Muslims who followed Ali ibn Abi Talib, also known as Ali, after the death of Muhammad. Ali is the cousin and son-in-law of Muhammad.

The foundation for the second-largest religion in the world was put forth by Muhammad in the Qur'an. "There are five major beliefs in Islam: there is only one God, there are angels, there have been many prophets but there is only one messenger, there will be a final judgment and it is possible to have knowledge of God and God's will."[30] More important than the five major beliefs are the five pillars of Islam, which are: there is no God but Allah, and Muhammad is his prophet; five prayers should be said daily facing Mecca in a prostrate posture; ritual almsgiving; a ritual fast during Ramadan; and a pilgrimage should be made to Mecca by every Muslim who is capable, at least once in their lifetime.

## Finding a Spokesperson

I was introduced to Najah Bazzy by an e-mail from Steve Spreitzer, who is the CEO of the Michigan Roundtable for Diversity and Inclusion. It took a few months for the two of us to get together. We met at the Zaman International Center. The center offers humanitarian services to the community. Najah, who is a registered nurse, is the founder and executive director of Zaman International. She has

---

[30] Frank S. Mead and Samuel S. Hill, *Handbook of Denominations in the United States 11th Edition*, revised by Craig D. Atwood (Nashville: Abington Press, 2001), 173.

also appeared on television numerous times in interdenominational groups, discussing the Muslim point of view. When I first met Najah, she was wearing a hijab and had a warm and friendly smile on her face. We went into her office, and I explained to her about the book I was putting together on how religions viewed god. Najah listened intently and offered to work on this book. The following is her essay entitled *"Bismillahee' Rahman Ar Raheem*; In the Name of God, Most Gracious, Most Merciful."

## By Najah Bazzy

Every action I take begins with this beautiful utterance, be it out loud, whispered, or silently in the voice of my heart. God goes by the name Allah. The God, he is unlimited and hard to fully grasp. Literally, the word means "the only one (to be worshipped)."

Allah is a genderless word. It is the word that God calls himself in the Jewish and Christian scriptures that predate the Islamic holy book called the Qur'an or the Recitation. Muslims from every background, in any language, use the name of Allah interchangeably with the word *God*. Arab Christians, in their traditional masses, use the word *Allah* as well. The ancient Aramaic language spoken by the divine messengers and prophets of God also used the word *Allah* to describe this incredible Creator.

I am a Muslim, one who submits to the concept of One Grand Creator. Islam is the name of the faith. It is made up of two Arabic root words that mean to "submit" and "peace."

The core concept of "peacefully submitting and submitting peacefully" through the intersection of my intellect, heart, and soul is what God/Allah wants of me and for me. Allah has created everything in the universe in a perfect order, which means that his perfection preceded the order. The idea of a perfect God, creating a perfectly ordered universe to submit to my needs and to my existence, leaves me in awe and wonderment. As I watch the night overtake the day and the day morph into the night, I feel the artwork of this perfect Creator. As I consider the orbit of the planets, the concept of gravity, rain, mountains, oceans, sand, grass, animals, plants, flowers, and all things that touch my senses and help me to exist, I feel God/Allah's reverence. The chemical elements, the concept of hydrogen and oxygen, the atom, and molecules are testimonies to his greatness. When I think of how these modalities exist so that I may exist, I feel God/Allah's mercy.

As a nurse, I work with the complexities of our human physical carry cases that we call our bodies. I have witnessed firsthand the birth of babies and their first breath. I have also witnessed the last breath of those who leave this existence to pass on to the next. I see miracles of the intellect and its ability to manufacture ideas that created advancement for the common good of humanity. In this I feel God/Allah's grace.

As a mother of four children, I have experienced the expansion of my heart's love every time a child was born. I understand that if I, in my limited capacity, can love my family so profoundly, then how must the Creator expand his love over all good things that please him. In this I feel God/Allah's all-encompassing love.

As a daughter who deeply loves her parents, I have respect for their station in life, their devotion and commitment to raising me and my siblings through poverty and prosperity and the sacrifices they made. In this I feel God/Allah's protection.

As an observant keeper of my home, I watched a bird for the entire month of Ramadan (the Muslim month of fasting), going back and forth, fetching the necessities to build her nest. I watched her with fascination and intrigue as she built the home for her eggs to be hatched. She did not build in a tree. She built her nest in a safe cove above the front door of my home. Every morning, I would stand and gaze in sheer amusement as she would fetch straw-like pieces and assemble them and then furnish her nest with feathers. I watched this strong bird hatch her eggs and fetch food. I watched her with full adoration and respect as she began to feed her offspring and give them flying lessons. I kept reflecting on

God/Allah's laws of equity and built-in survival modes for all that he makes. I would stand at the window and praise Allah several times a minute with great enthusiasm. The bird and I are moms, and we share a home. I was experiencing an empty-nest syndrome with all the kids off to college, and she was experiencing a full nest. I watched her every morning. In this I feel God/Allah's limitless compassion.

One day I was reading the Holy Qur'an and was reflecting on some of the verses. In one particular chapter called "The Thunder," (Raad, chapter 13), God says in a most poetic and beautiful verse that even the loud claps of thunder are singing his praise. Now when I hear thunder, my heart moves from the premise that the sky is angry to the premise that the sky is joyful. In this I feel God/Allah's majestic might.

Another verse of the Holy Qur'an, which we consider God/Allah's spoken word to humanity, comes in the chapter called "DayBreak," (Al Fajr, chapter 28). God in all his glory addresses the eternal human soul, which once created never dies. He says to us: "Oh You, Soul, Tranquil and Assured; Return to thy Lord Pleased, and well Pleasing, and Enter Then Ye, My Garden to dwell therein." In this I feel God/Allah's hospitality.

I have visited the holy city of Mecca in Saudi Arabia. There I performed one of the ritual rites prescribed upon all observing Muslims. It is a spiritual journey called the Hajj. There in Mecca one finds the first place that was created on earth and the house of worship built by Adam, and then reconstructed by Abraham and his son. We are asked to perform a circumambulation. This means going seven times around the holy shrine called the Ka'ba. In this motion a person is moving counterclockwise, walking with millions upon millions of people from every walk of life, each person with his or her own story, own tears, own supplications and prayers. Every person is dressed in the same type of clothing, equalizing our humanity. In these incredible moments, as all are focused and walking together in one direction, I get a glimpse of his ability to hear all the requests of his supplicants and respond in his own way. In this I feel God/Allah's diversity.

When I performed another ritual in the Hajj, I walked between two sacred mountains called Safa and Marwa. This is where Hagar, the second wife of Abraham, was left with her baby Ishmael to fend for themselves in the blazing sun of the Arabian Desert. Abraham cried as he left them per the command of God. God told Abraham through the great archangel Gabriel to leave them near the Sacred Ka'ba, and one day humanity would come from all four corners of the earth to pay respect to Hagar and her son Ishmael. Hagar ran between the two mountains, parched, begging God for help in a land devoid of water. God delivered his promise, and up from the ground sprang a freshwater geyser called Zam Zam. Zam Zam still runs till this day, as the freshwater that supplies the city of Mecca and its millions of visitors each year. In this I feel God/Allah's promise.

Another station in the pilgrimage to Mecca is a day's stay upon a plain called Arafat. Arafat is simply a large piece of land with significance for Muslims and humanity in general. Some historians believe that God reunited Adam and Eve after years of separation in which each roamed the earth on his or her own. The word *Arafat* in Arabic means where you may "come to know." In the Muslim tradition, anyone who stands on the plains of Arafat during the actual ritual Hajj will be forgiven of all sins and returned to a sinless state of being. We are taught through the Holy Qur'an that every believing man or woman will be sent an angel as the sun sets on Arafat, to whisper in their ear and heart that God sends his blessing and forgives you of all things big and small. In Arafat, I came to know myself, and I came to know my God/Allah as the host of my spiritual journey, the best and most gracious host. In this I feel God/Allah's mercy.

In another ritual, I traveled to a valley called Muzdalifa. In this land, I sat with millions of others under the five-star accommodations provided by God and God only. The earth is my resting place to sit, stand, walk, or lie down, and the star-studded sky is my light and lamp. Here I sat, pondered, reflected, and watched millions upon millions of people scattered across the land, camping for the night. In this I feel God/Allah's equity and awareness.

Following the valley stay in Muzdalifa, I traveled to a land called Mina. This is the land just outside of Mecca, where Abraham brought his son after having a dream in which God asked him to sacrifice his son. Abraham attempted to sacrifice his son, but the knife was ordered by God to become helpless. God sent to Abraham a ram to sacrifice instead of his son. In this I feel God/Allah's delivery of promise.

Either before or after the journey to Mecca, I am asked to visit the sacred burial site of my beloved prophet and messenger of God, Muhammad. May peace and blessings be upon him. In Medina, the city that houses his body, I breathe the pluralism of coexistence that occurred during the prophet's time there. I relish in a world where Muslims, Christians, Jews, and others lived as neighbors and coexisted with respect for their sacred texts. They lived as a monotheistic nation that embraced acceptance and tolerance with interfaith exchanges. In Medina, right next to the resting place of my beloved prophet and messenger of God, Muhammad, is a space no bigger than a ten-by-ten room. In this space is housed the prophet's *mimbar* (pulpit) and his *mihrab* (the cove he entered to pray). This sacred place is called Al Rowda. Muslims were taught by prophet Muhammad that whoever stands in Al Rowda has stood in heaven on earth. Millions flock to this area in the Prophet's Grand Mosque in Medina to pay their respect to the prophet of God and to pray. In this I feel God/Allah's serenity and tranquility.

Muslims are asked by God/Allah to pray five times a day. In this ritual experience, I stand and whisper my prayers. Then I bow as a slave would before a master. I then prostate my full body on the floor, placing my forehead on the ground, for I am groveling before the king of kings. In this I feel God/Allah's sovereignty.

I have been given a chance to stay up into the wee hours of the night to share with you my love of my faith and Creator. God says his greatest and most beloved creation is the intellect, because he commanded it to choose and differentiate. He taught it logic, reason, and deduction. He gave the intellect the ability to know him and accept him or the choice not to. He said there is no compulsion or force in religion. He wanted us to find him on our own and to come into a relationship with him free of fear and force. In this I feel God/Allah's servitude.

With the love of God in my heart, I feel gratitude and hope.

# Sikh

"Sikhism is the fifth largest religion in the world."[31] It "is a monotheistic religion, and the basic belief is represented in the phrase IK Onkar meaning One God."[32] Sikhism was founded in the fifteenth century by Guru Nanak Dev, partially because of his dislike of the caste system that was present in Hinduism. Sayings written by Guru Granth Sahib are the primary scripture used by the Sikhs. These sayings are thought of as the supreme spiritual authority. Their place of worship is called *gurdwara*, which means "gateway to the guru." Services may be led by either priests or members of the community. "Sikhs who have taken amrit,"[33] a ritual similar to baptism, follow five rules: *Kesh, Kangha, Kara, Kachera,* and *Kirpan*. Kesh is having long hair which has not been cut. It is covered by a turban. Men and women may keep their hair long. However, it is usually men who have long hair and wear a turban. Women who have long hair will only cover it when entering a gurdwara. Kangha means a small wooden comb which is used on the hair twice a day. "Kara is an iron bangle to be worn on the hand used most. A Kachera is a specific undergarment for men and women, and a Kirpan is a short dagger."[34]

---

[31] Jahnabi Baroosh, "Sikhism: Five Things to Know about the Sikh Religion," Last modified August 6, 2012, www.huffingtonpost.com/5-things-you-should-know-about-sikhism_n_1744657.ntm.

[32] Ibid.

[33] Ibid.

[34] Ibid.

## Finding a Spokesperson

I was introduced to Raman Singh through an e-mail sent by Steve Spreitzer, CEO of the Michigan Roundtable for Diversity and Inclusion. Raman and I met for the first time a number of months later at a diversity breakfast, when we sat at the same table. I explained to her about the project I was working on, and we set up another meeting at a later date. Raman is an attractive lady with a warm and friendly smile. She is a community activist and is also active in the Sikh community. When we met for the second time, Raman said she would contact Dr. Mandair, to see if he would write an essay about the Sikh's view of God. Later, Raman, Dr. Mandair, and I communicated by e-mail, and Dr. Mandair offered to write an essay. Dr. Arvind-Pal Mandair is a professor and has written a number of books on various aspects of the Sikh religion. He wrote the following essay titled "Who Is My God? A Sikh Perspective."

## By Dr. Arvind-Pal Mandair

"Who is 'my' God?" There is immediately a problem with this question. It seems so innocent, yet it presumes too much, not least that the language in which the question is asked is a neutral one, and the word *God* is universal, that it can be translated unproblematically across cultural and linguistic boundaries. We should remember that this language is the carrier of a Latinate consciousness that developed over many centuries through intimate contact with Christianity. In a sense the very first violence consists in presupposing that we are talking about the same thing, namely, "God."

In fact, the way the word *God* is used in the Abrahamic traditions is not the same as it is used in South Asian traditions (let alone the Chinese and other East Asian cultures). When used in this way ("Who is your God?"), it does not correspond to the actual nature of piety in Sikh devotion. Indeed, the nature of Sikh devotion cannot be understood in the Christian sense, since the latter presupposes a central definition of God's nature: that God exists and cannot *not* exist. And yet this definition of God is itself framed by a form of logic that is very specific to Western culture: logic of noncontradiction, the so-called law of noncontradiction.

Rather, to speak of Sikh piety or devotion, we must attend to the nature of an *experience*, rather than a presupposed universal term *God*. It is an experience that the founder of Sikhism speaks about prolifically. Guru Nanak simply speaks of the One (*ik*). This One is not a thing; it cannot be conceptualized in language as a "God," although different societies (and he was especially familiar with Hindu and Muslim societies) have had a tendency to do precisely this. According to Guru Nanak, if we are to speak of this experience of oneness as a feeling of an infinitely close presence, we can give this infinitely close presence an *infinite* variety of names such as Madho, Hari, Ram, and so on, thereby suggesting the experience is that idea of a personal god. At the same time, however, this very One is experienced as continually slipping away. Because of our finitude, we are unable to grasp it. It becomes absent in the very moment we say something positive about it, like a name or quality for instance. So the One, according to Nanak, is both absent and present at the same time.

But is this not a contradiction? How can anyone show devotion to an experience/One that is both there and not there? Guru Nanak's answer to this is deceptively simple. He suggests that the problem lies in the fact that our ordinary states of consciousness are unable to accept this contradiction, that we refuse to surrender to the contradiction. Instead we instinctively try to overcome the contradiction by objectivizing and polarizing the two aspects. For example, both Hindus and Muslims say that God is One, but they conceptualize this oneness in opposing ways. Whereas Hindus say that God is infinitely near to us and try to express his proximity through idols and images, Muslims regard this One as transcendent, infinitely beyond us. But neither *experiences* that One. This is why Guru Nanak said: "there is no Hindu, there is no Muslim"—implying that both miss the experience, which must include the other. As such they stopped *being* Hindu and Muslim. Instead both traditions began to emphasize the social projection of God, and through these social projections, pitted themselves against each other.

For Guru Nanak, this social projection was nothing more than the anxiety of a deluded ego. in contrast, Guru Nanak emphasizes that to attain the experience of the One, the devotee should focus not on God but on that which at the same time *prevents* the experience and is the very *means* of the experience: the ego, mind, or self. So Guru Nanak suggests a more workable formula by asking the devotee to keep in mind that *God (or the experience of the One) and ego cannot be in the same place at the same time.*

Listen to what Both Nanak and Kabir say on this issue:

Nanak:
When I act in ego, you're not present.
When you're present, no ego can be present.
O Nanak, repeat these words: "He is me, I'm him,"
The one in whom the three worlds are merged.

Kabir:
When I am, Hari is not.
Now Hari is, and I am no more.
By saying "You, You," I have become you.
"I am" is in me no longer.

Judging from what both Nanak and Kabir say, the heart of the problem seems to be that we are socially conditioned to live, think, and act only on the basis of ego ("when I am, I act in ego"). Yet there is something in the very structure of this ego that prevents us from experiencing oneness. (You're not there / Hari is not.) To undergo the experience, the ego needs to be absent. One has to struggle with it and yet remain within the world. This is no easy task. In fact Nanak likens it to crossing a mighty ocean in a small raft. But he also says that the means for achieving this is within reach of everyone without exception. We all have the capability to achieve that sovereign experience, indeed to become sovereign, free.

This basic insight—that attainment of a sovereign consciousness, perfection, or what Guru Nanak called the state of *gurmukh*—is everyone's birthright. It is ingrained into the nature of the self and attainable through transformation of our everyday consciousness. Most importantly, for Sikhs, it is necessary to protect everyone else's access to this wellspring of life and creativity. The desire to protect others' access to the creative source of life, to the possibility of living creatively, rather than in fear, remains the focus of Sikh devotion, the wellspring from which it draws sustenance.

# Sunni Muslim/Islam

Sunnis are Muslims who followed Abdullah ibn Abi Quhaafah, also known as Abu Bakr, after the death of Muhammad. Abu Bakr was the father-in-law of Muhammad and one of his advisors.

The foundation for the second-largest religion in the world was put forth by Muhammad in the Qur'an. "There are five major beliefs in Islam: there is only one God, there are angels, there have been many prophets but there is only one messenger, there will be a final judgment and it is possible to have knowledge of God and God's will."[35] More important than the five major beliefs are the five pillars of Islam, which are: there is no God but Allah, and Muhammad is his prophet; five prayers should be said daily facing Mecca in a prostrate posture; ritual almsgiving; a ritual fast during Ramadan; and a pilgrimage should be made to Mecca by every Muslim who is capable, at least once in their lifetime.

## An Interview with Imam Steve Mustapha Elturk

Imam Elturk was another religious leader I was introduced to by an e-mail from Steve Spreitzer, CEO for the Michigan Roundtable for Diversity and Inclusion. I met with Imam Elturk at the mosque in which he officiates. He made me feel extremely comfortable in interviewing him. The following is Imam Elturk's interview titled "Who is My God?"

---

[35] Frank S. Mead and Samuel S. Hill, *Handbook of Denominations in the United States 11th Edition*, revised by Craig D. Atwood (Nashville: Abington Press, 2001), 173.

Who is my God? There is nothing like unto him, unimaginable, incomprehensible, yet he is there. He is responsible for the whole universe and beyond.

Since the dawn of man, people have grappled with the question, does God exist? Many discussions have revolved around the existence of God, and many people, using their intellect and reason, have tried to prove the existence or nonexistence of God.

Regarding the existence of God, it could not have been put better than a nomad's answer. He said, "Don't camel droppings point to a camel, don't footprints on the sand tell of a traveler, and don't the stars in the sky, the mountains, the trees, and everything else point to a maker?" This maker is God Almighty, the creator of everything. He is sublime, transcendent, and there is nothing like unto him. He is beyond our imagination.

From an Islamic perspective, he is a personal God. Not in the same way we perceive a human person with hands and arms and head. Despite the verse, "I created him [Adam] with My own two hands." "I hear," he says. "I see," he says. He, however, does not see and hear with eyes and ears like our eyes and ears. How he sees and hears, we cannot fathom. He is not like us; there is nothing like unto him. Whatever comes to mind about him regarding his being or essence is beyond our stretch of imagination.

His attributes that were communicated to us through his scriptures and prophets give us an idea as to the persona of God.

Firstly, he is kind and benevolent, compassionate and merciful. There are 114 chapters in the Qur'an. With the exception of one, all begin with, "In the name of God (Allah) the most compassionate, the ever merciful." In the Arabic language, it is *al-Rahman, al-Rahim*. They both mean basically the same, "mercy" or "compassion." The patterns, however, on which the root of mercy are formed, al-Rahman, and al-Rahim, express intensity and continuity respectively. Therefore, al-Rahman, al-Rahim, mean that his mercy is very potent and continuous. My God is extremely and continuously compassionate and merciful. Nothing in this world will change these attributes.

Secondly, God is very powerful. He is so powerful that he deserves to be worshipped. He is so powerful that he can do anything he wants. People's power is limited, and people can only create things from existing materials. My God is so powerful that he can create anything he wants out of absolute nothingness. All he has to do is say "Be," and it will be.

The spirits in the souls of human beings came by his command, and they came at a time when there was nothing—nothing in this world, nothing in the universe, no angels, absolutely nothing except him. I can't remember that because I was not there with the senses I have today, but I was there in spirit. I have been reminded of this through my book (the Qur'an) in which my prophet (Muhammad, peace be upon him) delivered this profound and revolutionary message to me. Muhammad received it from archangel Gabriel, who brings down messages from God, the Creator, to his apostles, and the apostles would give these messages to the people, the created.

We were told in the scripture that we (all humans, past, present, and future) were once, in the form of spirits, in front of God Almighty, and he took a covenant from us testifying that he is our Lord. He then put us here on earth to fulfill that covenant. This taught me that it is God, my Lord, whom I should depend on for all of my affairs and needs, physical and spiritual. When one reaches that stage of truly believing in the existence of God and in his power, that he is in control and in charge, and that he is the sustainer, the most kind and compassionate Lord who looks after you and guides you; when one reaches this stage and unconditionally surrenders to him, only then will one begin to have a state of inner peace and tranquility that no amount of money or material things can buy.

Most if not all of us must have asked ourselves at one time or another, who is God? Or does God exist? This is quite natural and part of man's curiosity to know and inquire about things, visible and unseen. This is the superiority of humans over all animals and other creations, the ability to use his or her *super* intellect that God has exclusively given to humans. All the knowledge we have, the physical knowledge in this physical world, has come from one source, and that is God Almighty.

The first word given to Muhammad was *read*.

> Read in the name of your Lord who created
> Created man out of a hanging substance (clot)
> Read and your Lord is most bountiful
> It is He who taught the use of the pen
> It is He who taught man that which he knew not.
> (Qur'an 96:1–5)

If you trace all knowledge back, it had to have started somewhere. It can be traced back to Adam and Eve, from whom we came. We are all brothers and sisters in humanity—Jews, Christians, Buddhists, Sikhs, Muslims—all the people of different shades and colors and tongues belong to one family, and that is Adam and Eve. We are all really brothers and sisters.

Adam had to be responsible for all of this knowledge, and there is a verse in the Qur'an that says, "God taught Adam the names of all things." We are now growing at an accelerated rate of knowledge. If people would only recognize who is behind all of this knowledge and be grateful, our condition would be different today.

This is my Lord; he is kind and compassionate. He deserves to be honored. He demands to be worshipped, and he deserves to be worshipped.

He hears everything, and he responds. Once you know him, you'll love him. He becomes your friend. He is a kind and loving God. He is not someone to be afraid of. The only thing people should be afraid of is the consequences of their bad actions and deeds.

Once you reach that complete belief in God, you are on top of the world. You are there for God, as he is there for you. You remember him, he remembers you. You come to him walking, he comes to you running.

There is a verse that says, "Call on Allah, or al-Rahman, whichever name you call Him [by], to Him belong all the beautiful names."

We have ninety-nine names for him that are not only names but also attributes that describe his being. The following verses demonstrate some of these attributes.

> God is He save whom there is no deity: the One who knows all that is beyond the reach of a created being's perception, as well as all that can be witnessed by a creature's senses or mind: He, the Most Gracious, the Dispenser of Grace.
>
> God is He save whom there is no deity: the Sovereign Supreme, the Holy, the One with whom all salvation rests, the Giver of Faith, the One who determines what is true and false, the Almighty, the One who subdues wrong and restores right, the One to whom all greatness belongs! Utterly remote is God, in His limitless glory, from anything to which men may ascribe a share in His divinity!
>
> He is God, the Creator, the Maker who shapes all forms and appearances! His [alone] are the attributes of perfection. All that is in the heavens and on earth extols His limitless glory: for He alone is almighty, truly wise! (Qur'an 59:21–23).

Most people believe in him, but they do not have a personal connection with him. They lack conviction.

Most believers do believe in God. However, the only time they remember God is when they are sick or in trouble. Many people live a hypocritical life, thinking they believe in God, but they really don't know who God is. People need to know him. We know him by how he describes himself to us. We have the Qur'an, his final word that hasn't been changed or altered, that describes to us who my God is.

We go through cycles of ups and downs of life. A true servant of God always praises and is grateful to his Lord during times of prosperity, and you find him patient at times of adversity, waiting for relief. Just as there is always sunshine after rain, there is always ease after difficulty. You know that you are being subject to a great trial.

God is one and alone, and there is no other. He has no partners and needs no one. God does not depend on anything. He is absolutely independent, and it is we who are dependent on him. He is constantly there. He knows the counts of every leaf on every tree in the world. Not a single leaf falls without seeking permission from him. That's how great he is.

I do believe in science; once everything was formed, the entire cosmos runs in perfect harmony. How could that be? Someone has to be responsible for that. I believe God created everything with a purpose. He is all-powerful, he is with us wherever we are, and he sees everything.

There is another side of his majesty: he gets upset. He does not like to see injustice. It is not one of his traits; it is not one of his attributes. Man is given free will and is doing wrong and injustice to none but himself. That is why God sent human messengers over the centuries to help us decide what is right and what is wrong, in the hope we follow the right and leave the wrong.

God Almighty is watching, and he is guiding. He guides those who want to be guided to the right path and misguides those who want to be led astray. He helps those who seek his help while leaving others alone. But there will come a time when he will have to deal with them all, and this is what we call the day of judgment. A verse in the Qur'an states, "We belong to God and to him is our return." I personally believe, as is my faith, that we will all die and resurrect before our Lord, the Lord of everyone. There is no such thing as *his* Lord, *your* Lord, and *my* Lord. We have one Lord; we have one God. He is the creator of this whole universe, the one and only, the first and the last, the one in which there is nothing like unto him.

> All that is in the heavens and on earth extols God's limitless glory: for He alone is almighty, truly wise! His is the dominion over the heavens and the earth; He grants life and deals death; and He has the power to will anything. He is the First and the Last, and the apparent, and the hidden: and He has full knowledge of everything (Qur'an 57:1–3).

That's my God.

# *Unitarian Universalist*

The Unitarian Universalist Church was formed in 1961 by the merger of the Universalist Church of America and the Unitarian Association. Each church associated with this religion believes that God is the source of mind and spirit. However, each church has the right to vary in its belief structure. Other areas the churches have in common are that they believe in the worth of every human being, that the search for truth uses all prophets, Jesus is a great prophet, and the Bible is a collection of religious writings. They also believe science is a source of knowledge, justice and peace are the goals for all actions, the world community should be based on brotherhood, and prayer will lift the mind beyond the ordinary.

### Finding a Spokesperson

I met with Reverend Riegal a couple of times over a few months, at the church in which he officiates. On my first meeting with Reverend Riegal, I was impressed by his relaxed demeanor and kindness. I explained the book I was working on, and he offered to become part of it. In reading his sermon, I am sure you will see that Reverend Riegal has thought about God in depth. The following is Reverend Alex Riegal's sermon titled "A Dream within a Dream."

### By Reverend Alexander Riegal

I stand amid the roar
Of a surf-tormented shore,
And I hold within my hand

Grains of the golden sand —
How few! Yet how they creep
Through my fingers to the deep,
While I weep — while I weep!
O God! can I not grasp
Them with a tighter clasp?
O God! can I not save
One from the pitiless wave?
Is all that we see or seem
But a dream within a dream?

— Edgar Allan Poe

In past sermons you have heard me speak about the ground of being, that sense of the greater reality in which each of us grounds ourselves, and which for each of us takes a different form. This ground of being I refer to as Go-B, a substitute catchall term intended to help us acknowledge that no matter how we conceive of it, there is a greater reality in which each of us "lives and moves and has our being," to steal a theological phrase. For some of us, Go-B is Go-d, a supreme, transcendent being that is the source of our existence and upon which our lives depend. For others of us Go-B is the material cosmos that has somehow — wonderfully, majestically, and mysteriously — brought about humankind as a conscious epiphenomenon within itself ("epiphenomenon" here simply meaning a happenstance result of the initial phenomenon of the material cosmos). And for others of us, Go-B is the human community, in which we find a deep sense of belonging and meaning in life.

I believe that in my preaching I've emphasized the value of human community and the wonder of the material cosmos, but I don't believe I have ever laid out my specific thoughts about God. I have, in fact, talked about my position as a mystical humanist, by which I mean a spiritual delving into the mystery of existence, tempered by a strong ethical foundation. Yet specifics about God have admittedly been lacking. Indeed, I've been very good at skirting the issue, mostly because I believe that it's the way we are in relationship with one another that is the most important question in the religious life, but also because in my experience having conversations about God in the midst of a bunch of UUs [Unitarian Universalists] is like tossing a steak into the middle of a pack of starving Rottweilers. As soon as the subject comes up, we bare our rational teeth and mentally tear the topic asunder, leaving it on the ground in a heap of semantic shreds. It can be a very disquieting experience and one not one many people wish to risk.

Nevertheless, this question of God recurs over and over again, even in our UU circles, where it is so problematic. I think this is because even though most everyone in UU circles would admit that how we are in relationship with one another is the most important question in the religious life, we all still have this deep, existential need to know what is ultimate. In other words, as each of us struggles to figure out what Go-B is for us, we find that this struggle necessarily includes the question of God. So for what it's worth, I'll offer my thoughts on the matter this morning, in hopes that they might be grist for your theological mill, but also in hopes that it will help return some respectability to the question of God in UU circles, or at least *this* UU circle.

My thoughts about the question of God have changed throughout my life and will continue to do so. That's one of the reasons I'm a Unitarian Universalist. As a UU my personal theology is allowed to evolve over time, which is part of what it means to take part in a "living tradition." So realize that what you're getting this morning is a snapshot of where I am now, based on my current thinking and certain experiences I've had in my spiritual practice.

In the Western world (our heritage), we have been witness to a profound and sometimes vicious conflict between religion and science. This conflict is rooted in the fact that religion is about belief and faith, whereas science is about reason and evidence. I don't think it's necessary to explain that belief and faith often conflict with reason and evidence. But what it is necessary to explain is how often that conflict is rooted in obstinacy rather than contradiction. Let me give you a couple of examples of how this is the case with *each* side of the debate.

We are all very familiar with the debate between evolutionists and proponents of intelligent design (the belief that certain features of the universe, most especially conscious life-forms, are best explained by invoking an Intelligent Designer rather than the process of natural selection). The people who hold to intelligent design do so against a preponderance of evidence to the contrary, such as the fossil record, which adequately explains how natural selection can give rise to conscious life-forms without invoking an intelligent cause behind it all—that is, God. Such tenacious adherence to an explanation that flies in the face of evidence is sheer obstinacy. (I feel I should note here that by affirming natural selection, one does not thereby negate God per se, but only a certain idea of God, which brings me to my second example.)

For its part, the scientific refutation of God is a refutation of a straw God, that is, a very specific and limited idea of God. The idea of God that science tends to set up as a target of attack tends to be the traditional Western, monotheistic, patriarchal, miracle-working God revealed in Western sacred scripture: the Jewish Bible, the Koran, and the New Testament. The refutation of this God, especially on scientific grounds, is easy to acquire—witness Richard Dawkins. The notion of God that comes to us from the East, however, is never allowed to be part of the conversation. That is a God of a very different sort, and until science addresses the possibility that a more Eastern idea of God might in fact be tenable, even given, or *especially* given scientific understanding, its refutation of God per se is dubious at best. Its tenacious adherence to the straw God is another example of sheer obstinacy.

It seems to me that our culture is stuck between two relatively obstinate forces that are so bent on winning the debate regarding the question of God that the rest of us, stuck in the middle, are not benefiting from any meaningful dialogue concerning the matter. We are not being led to any deeper understanding of the question and indeed have become so frustrated that virtually none of us is listening to the proponents on either side of the debate. Instead we are left to our own intuition and creative devices to create our own theological positions in a world where belief and faith, reason and evidence seem incapable of even recognizing one another. Thus, we wander through the technological age draped in rather shabby theological garb. We are poor spirits in a rich materialistic age. To overcome this problem it is time to overcome the obstinacy that has become entrenched in the debate between religion and science. For this to happen, two things are required.

First, for the question of God to be meaningfully addressed, especially from a scientific perspective, we have to be willing to consider other ideas of God aside from the less tenable traditional Western, monotheistic, patriarchal, miracle-working God revealed in Western sacred scripture. We must consider notions of the divine as they appear in the East; in Hinduism, Buddhism, and Taoism. As is said in the Tao Te Ching, "The Tao that can be spoken is not the eternal Tao." In other words, the ground of being is beyond human comprehension and expression. There is a similar notion in Hinduism, in which God is thought of as *nirguna-brahman,* the ground of being without form or name. Even further, in Buddhism there is not so much a notion of the divine as much as a rejection of the divine and an affirmation of universal consciousness as the ground of being. In short, these ideas of God are very different than the traditional Western idea of God and do not lead us into the same types of less tenable claims and conclusions. Unfortunately I don't have time this morning to construct an Eastern notion of the divine at a very deep level—that's another sermon for another time—but the gist of it is that these Eastern notions of the divine are more tenable from a scientific perspective and need to be considered in this debate.

The second thing that needs to happen for us to overcome the debate between religion and science is for science to recognize that its critique of religion, and specifically the question of God, is grounded in an older scientific model that is no longer considered to be the only viable scientific model. Indeed, from the perspective of quantum physics, science finds itself having a very different orientation toward the question of God, at least if we consider God according to Eastern models. This is mostly what I want to focus on for the remainder of the sermon, because I think it's an important point that many scientists who ridicule religion, and especially belief in God, tend to ignore. It is science's most profound example of selective thinking.

The older scientific method was founded on Newtonian physics. Regarding it there are two important points for us to remember. First, Newtonian physics worked from the basic proposition that the fundamental stuff of the universe is matter. That means that at the most fundamental level, *everything* in existence is ultimately reducible to matter. Second, from this proposition it follows that consciousness arises *from* matter. Consciousness is said to be an epiphenomenon of the biological animal, which means that consciousness is a *secondary quality* within the cosmos.

Toward the beginning of the last century, a group of scientists were establishing the field that is now known as quantum physics. There are two important points about their endeavor that are important for us this morning. First they discovered, in a nutshell, that all matter is comprised of energy vibrating at different frequencies. This undermined the basic proposition of Newtonian physics, the notion that the fundamental stuff of the universe is matter. Second, and most profoundly, they recognized that in the quantum world there was a particular problem known as the measurement problem.

Specifically, the measurement problem is the problem that in the quantum world all that exists are possible states of things. It is not until one observes a phenomenon that any of these possible states occurs. The best example of this problem is the thought experiment known as Schrödinger's cat, but there isn't time to explain that this morning, so let me try something simpler. In a nutshell, an atom is actually spread out all over the place (like a spread-out wave), that is, until one observes it. It is this act of observation that actually causes it to appear in a particular place. The conclusion drawn from this is that *the observer plays a vital role in determining the outcome of events*.

For our purposes this morning, that means the following: Since the outcome of events is dependent upon observation, then consciousness, not matter, is the fundamental stuff of the universe. Let me repeat that: *Since the outcome of events is dependent upon observation, then consciousness, not matter, is the fundamental stuff of the universe.*

So quantum physics has undermined the older Newtonian model, at least at the subatomic level. It has shown us that energy, not matter, is the fundamental stuff of the universe. More importantly, it has shown us that consciousness is not a *secondary quality* within the cosmos but the primary quality within the cosmos. That is, quantum physics seems to point us to the conclusion that consciousness is the fundamental stuff of the universe, the ground of being. The reason this is significant is that this conclusion matches Eastern ideas of the divine. Consciousness as the fundamental stuff of the universe is directly in line with Buddhist, Hindu, and Taoist ideas of God.

Indeed, so closely wedded are Eastern ideas of God and the quantum world that outside of the CERN Laboratory in Switzerland, the home of quantum physics, stands a large statue of Shiva Nataraj, the Hindu deity that represents the divine cosmic dance of creation and destruction. On the plaque beneath his feet are inscribed these words, from Fritjof Capra's book, *The Tao of Physics*:

> Modern physics has shown that the rhythm of creation and destruction is not only manifest in the turn of the seasons, and in the birth and death of all living creatures, but is also the very essence of inorganic matter ... For the modern physicists, then, Shiva's dance is the dance of subatomic matter.

> Hundreds of years ago, Indian artists created visual images of dancing Siva in a beautiful series of bronzes. In our time, physicists have used the most advanced technology to portray the patterns of the cosmic dance. The metaphor of the cosmic

dance thus unifies ancient mythology, religious art, and modern physics.

So what does all of this tell us about the question of God? I think it tells us that the age-old debate between science and religion, between belief and faith and reason and evidence, is surpassable. It even tells us that belief in God is an entirely tenable position to hold, even from a scientific viewpoint. But it's important to note here that finding belief in God tenable from a scientific viewpoint is a far different matter than finding evidence for the existence of God on scientific grounds. Actual evidence for the existence of God must come from something *other* than a scientific theory that renders belief in God *tenable*. It must come from personal, subjective experience that renders God actual.

This is immediately problematic, however, because personal, subjective experience can never be taken to be proof for anyone but the person having the experience. (As the old idiom says, "To those who have had the experience, no explanation is necessary. To those who have not had the experience, no explanation is possible.") So the best we can do regarding the question of God, beyond gaining scientific knowledge that makes belief in God tenable, is prove the fact of God to ourselves alone. How do we do this? Is it even possible? Let me very briefly touch upon this, but again, this, too, is another sermon for another time.

The short answer is that for thousands of years, mystics have been searching for God through various spiritual methods. They tell us they have found God through some of these methods. Even further, they have given us their methodology for discovering God ourselves. It is through the method of the mystics, then, that we have the *possibility* of attaining a personal, subjective experience that renders God actual, at least for us personally. In other words, if we walk the path that the mystics prescribe, measure our spiritual experiences against their reports, and guide ourselves by the limited knowledge we have (which I've discussed in this sermon), we have a very good foundation for delving into the mystery, for exploring this question of God.

This is part of what I'm doing with my own spiritual practice, namely, exploring the question of God through various spiritual practices. I have taken on the methods the mystics prescribe, and I have had certain experiences that seem to corroborate their claims, at least so far. This doesn't mean that I draw their same conclusions, at least not yet. But, it certainly makes it hard to discount them. So for me the journey continues. I don't know where I'll be tomorrow regarding this question of God. But I do know this, at least for myself: belief in God is an entirely tenable position to hold, and the possibility of God certainly remains.

# *Wiccan/Pagan*

The basic theology of the Wiccan/pagan religion is that the planet is a single living organism called Mother Earth. The religion looks for the maximum potential in people. Individuals can reach this potential by having a spiritual relationship with Mother Earth, through the realization of ultimate individual freedom, and taking personal responsibility that is harmonious with Mother Earth.

## Finding a Spokesperson

My search for Wiccans led me to a metaphysical store. After going there a few times, I could not get anyone to follow through on this project. I then started to research Wiccans and came across Julie, an ordained high priestess. We talked on the phone a couple of times and then met at a coffee shop. I told her about the book I was putting together. Julie discussed her background and agreed to work on the project. The following is Julie's essay titled "A Wiccan Prayer for Peace."

## By Julie McGowan

As a multidenominational minister and ordained high priestess, I draw from many traditions and religious beliefs in my practice. I have officiated marriages, performed last rites, and prayed with people of all faiths. What I pray for most often is peace.

My own initiation into the "craft" was inspired by my personal longing to find the "divine feminine" that had somehow been mysteriously left out of all the formal religious teachings I had encountered as a child. I felt called from a very young age to serve the world and know God more closely, while at the same time painfully aware of my lot as a young woman, unable to ever rise to a leadership position within the confines of the Catholic faith. At the age of thirteen, I told my father I would no longer attend Mass until someone could give me a viable reason for the lack of women in leadership positions within the church.

I struggled to find my own way. I missed the smell of incense, the lighting of candles, and the ritual Sunday Mass. I prayed for guidance. I sensed other people's energy, interpreted dreams, and began to channel information from a place beyond what our five senses and our three-dimensional minds could explain. I felt the steady presence of the Virgin Mary with me through the whole process, as she was my first encounter with the divine feminine. Suddenly I began to see the whole world as my church, every breath as a prayer, and all things alive with the same energy that coursed through my veins. This is when the veil was lifted, and I knew it was time to answer the calling that had been growing ever louder within my heart. My calling was to use the gifts I had been given to assist in healing myself and others. This was fascinating and frightening to those around me, and I quickly learned that my "gift" was not to be shared openly, save for a few close individuals.

My mother gave me my first set of tarot cards when I was fifteen years old. My father warned me not to "dabble in the occult." I took his advice seriously and learned how to shield myself from harm as I began to study astrology, folklore, and ancient religions. I discovered that the "divine feminine" had been strategically erased from many of the sacred texts today's mainstream religions draw from. Popular culture's longstanding ideas about witchcraft as a religion synonymous with devil worship are inaccurate. The word *occult* simply means "hidden." When I read tarot cards for others, I remind them that they are in charge of their own destiny. My intention is to reveal what has been hidden, in order to empower the individual and the collective. I can "see" what obstacles lie in their way and what wounds are in need of tending to, but it is ultimately up to them to walk their own path.

So what is God/Goddess according to a practitioner of the Wiccan faith? God is an energy that is immanent in all things. Rather than a finite entity, God/Goddess is understood to be inherent in all genders, races, classes, and species, both living and nonliving. Because God/Goddess is an energy, it goes on infinitely, ceaselessly, changing forms. The Goddess has been called by many names and was predominantly thought of as a sacred mother and ruler of the forces of nature that give and receive life. The God was thought of as the hunter/warrior/father that provided protection and sustenance. The differentiation between God and Goddess in the craft are not necessary gendered definitions set in binary opposition to one another, as God/Goddess are intrinsically one. The craft has leaders and scholars, high priests and priestesses, although without formal hierarchical structure, as God/Goddess speaks and moves through all things equally. Elders are shown respect according to their experiences and the acquisition of knowledge, rather than their age alone. Leadership within the craft is meant to facilitate "empowerment of every individual" rather than "power over another."

The practice of witchcraft takes on many forms and draws from many traditions accordingly. Practitioners themselves use varying terms to describe their religious identity, including shaman, warlock, pagan, druid, and Wiccan. The word *witch* comes from the Indo-European root word *"wick"* or *"weik"* which means "to bend or shape." A witch is simply one who chooses to consciously bend or shape his or her reality through ritual. Magic is defined by those in the craft as the act of sending energy/prayer through a symbol. Just as Buddhists use prayer beads for meditation or a Catholic uses a rosary, a witch uses a cauldron, a broom, a wand, a candle, or a crystal to send energy through. Ceremonial magic, where one calls upon the elements of earth, fire, water, and air to assist in bringing about a specific outcome, has its roots in various indigenous practices all over the world.

A pentacle, a five-pointed star with a circle around it, has been a sacred symbol for those who practice magic. The five points of the star stand for earth, fire, water, air, and spirit, while the circle represents the cosmos. These two together represent the juxtaposition of spirit and matter, sacred and profane, immanent and transcendent. A cauldron represents the womb, where new beginnings occur and take shape. The three legs of the cauldron represent harmony and balance of body, mind, and spirit. Many witches use a blade, sword, or dagger in ceremony to ritually sever ties with those things that restrict their freedom or happiness or to inscribe symbols that empower them individually. A broom is another common symbol associated with witches and is used to symbolically clear a space in preparation for prayer or ritual.

A witch acknowledges the forces of nature and his or her place in nature through ceremony. A practitioner draws upon the cycles of life/death/rebirth, the changing phases of the moon, and the wheel of the year. Many Wiccans celebrate four Sabbats in addition to the thirteen full moons that turn the year's wheel. The Sabbats are holy days such as the autumn and spring equinoxes, when the hours of sunlight are in perfect balance with the hours of darkness; the summer solstice, which marks the longest day of sunlight; and the winter solstice, which marks the longest day of darkness. A ceremonial celebration usually consists of gathering in a circle, calling in the elemental forces, raising the energy through song or prayer, grounding or binding the energy, and closing the circle with the sharing of food. The practice of ritual magic has no concrete rules and is open to the individual's creative freedom, although many practitioners are mindful of the basic universal law of reciprocity in ritual. When invoking magic, one must bear in mind that whatever is sent out comes back in threefold. It is important, therefore, to be vigilant about one's own intentions. Ritual magic that is used in a harmful or malevolent way will cause harm to those who invoke it, while ritual magic that is intended to heal and help others will also heal and help those who invoke it.

While there are some practitioners of the craft who have abused their power and harmed others, it is important to acknowledge that in every faith, there are those extreme few who deviate and become bad apples that spoil the whole bushel. It is important to pray for them. The cries of more than sixty thousand women throughout history in Europe and the Americas who were hunted and executed for their beliefs still echo in my ears today. I pray for them, as well as the executioners, for they are all my brothers and sisters.

Many witches today still face religious persecution and therefore choose to remain "in the broom closet" as a result. I choose to speak openly about my beliefs, with the intention of clearing up common misconceptions, opening up a dialogue with others, and building a bridge between those of varying faiths, so that we can collectively create the peace I continue to pray so diligently for. We are at the turning point in human history where our technology has advanced to such a degree that the push of a button could end all life on earth as we know it. It is time for our hearts to evolve and catch up to our minds, so the technology available to us is used in ways that heal, empower, and sustain life. This requires forgiveness and respect of those who are walking a different path than your own. It means becoming more committed with every word you speak, every breath you take, and every thought that passes through your mind. We are on this planet together, and our very survival depends upon it.

# Zen Buddhism

There are many different forms of Buddhism. Buddhism was started by Siddhartha Gautama, who was born a prince in 560 BCE. When he was thirty-one years old, he began searching for the meaning of life. Six years after meeting with many different Indian religious groups, he sat under a tree and meditated. The tree became known as the tree of enlightenment, and Siddhartha Gautama became known as the Enlightened One, or Buddha. He taught the dharma, meaning the true way of life. The dharma is made up of four tenets called the four truths and the eightfold path, which is in the shape of a wheel. The dharma is followed by all Buddhists: all existence entails suffering; the cause of suffering is desire; the way to escape suffering is to rid oneself of desire; and to be emancipated from desire, one must follow the eightfold path. The eightfold path consists of the right understanding, resolve, speech, conduct, livelihood, effort, attention, and concentration. Zen Buddhism is a mystical form of Buddhism that was founded in China. It has two different techniques for meditation. One is based on an anecdotal event given by the master for the students to solve; this is called the *koan* and is used by the Lin-Chi school of thought. The other uses the doctrine of silent illumination, and that process is called the Ts'ao-tung school of thought. The Zen Buddhist community in the United States is led by Westerners.

Finding a Spokesperson

I met with Anzen Melanie Davenport at the Zen Buddhist Temple in Detroit. Anzen Melanie was unpretentious and pleasant as she invited me into the kitchen at the temple. We sat at the table in the kitchen and drank tea while I talked and she listened. I explained the question I was asking religious leaders, the one in which they define their God. Anzen Melanie thought about the question and then agreed to participate in the book. The following is Anzen Melanie Davenport's essay.

## By Anzen Melanie Davenport

The question "Who is your God?" in Buddhism is best answered by another question — "What God?" The teachings in this tradition are full of wonderful paradoxes, so I'll explain why such an issue is best answered by another question.

Zen Buddhism, the religion I'm formally ordained in, is often described for better or worse as atheistic or not a really a religion at all, which is not altogether true. Buddhism offers the same things other religions do for the community: regular public services and ceremonies, liturgy, scripture, holidays, a set of organized behaviors, moral structure, and an established clergy. Conversely, most religions are founded upon or require a belief in a creator god, and Buddhism just doesn't offer that.

The historical Buddha, Shakyamuni, taught that this thing we call life, in all its forms, has an unthinkable beginning and no visible end — and ostensibly no creator ... at least, not a creator we could *ever* begin to define with our tiny human brains and limited vocabulary. As he traveled the Indian subcontinent, teaching for the better part of eighty years, he was probably asked this question repeatedly. Based on some of his earlier teachings in the Pali Canon, there are probably three good reasons why the Buddha refused to make an official statement about the existence of a divine creator:

1. In the midst of life with all of its fears, hopes, joys, and disappointments, people wanted a spiritual anchor they could put in their pocket and cling to in the hopes that it would not change.

2. Some would take the spiritual anchor and use it to engage in excessive metaphysical meandering and never actually integrate their spiritual beliefs into everyday life.
3. People wanted that spiritual anchor as confirmation of their own beliefs about how life should work. Eventually some people would hit others over the head with that anchor by starting wars with them if they didn't follow their beliefs.

And we know these things are still going on, right? Ultimately every human goes through these particular stages of spiritual discovery. Some of us just tend to get stuck in one stage or another for a while. And some of us get stuck our whole lives.

Shakyamuni Buddha even dodged his own followers' attempts to deify him. At the end of his life, he advised his followers to "be refuges unto yourselves, seeking no external refuge." This simply means trusting in your own innate wisdom and experience to guide you throughout life. The prescribed method of getting to know your own true nature in this tradition is through meditation. Through our practice, we get to experience the wisdom that goes beyond words and concepts in a more intimate way, rather than supplicating to a God that supposedly exists elsewhere.

With that said, Buddhist traditions do acknowledge the existence of other planes of reality, and scores of teachings mention spirits and godlike beings that can assist followers on their journey toward enlightenment. However, these beings are just as impermanent as we are; they are also subject to wheel of birth and death. Belief in gods, bodhisattvas, spirits, and demigods are neither compulsory nor problematic in Buddhism; the tradition has a long history of integrating gods and customs from every culture the practice takes root in. It is worth considering that the gods, bodhisattvas, and spirits may only exist as forms of our collective unconscious. This, of course, is a theory and is subject to change!

"Spiritual practice in Buddhism is ultimately not about finding a God to worship. What is most important in our practice is giving up our ideas about how everything should work (including God) so that we can serve the world just as it is, from a place of compassion and clarity."

# Who Is God?

Some people perceive that there is no God. Their opinion is that the idea itself is one promulgated by people to help them feel better about their world. Others see God as an it, he, or he/she. The ones who see God as a he or he/she tend to personify their almighty. They give their God humanlike characteristics. These personality traits are the ones they relate to and ask for help from. The people who see God as an it see God as something that is all around us and cannot be described. This thought is in concurrence with all who worship, even if they personify God. Their opinion is that God is all around us and has control of all our surroundings, thoughts, and feelings.

So if God is all around us and is always willing to help us and others, then why do individuals have disdain for people who do not worship their God? In my opinion, this is because of a form of religious nationalism in which each religion perceives their God as "the best." This thought is based on tribalism, in which each tribe perceives themselves to be the strongest, boldest, most mighty, and all-controlling. The problem with the aforementioned is that it does not fit into the perception of God. If God is a kind, caring being who wishes no harm to humankind, then how can God make the statement that the different ways of viewing God cannot be tolerated? Especially since God may be all around us and involved in all aspects of humankind.

Therefore, the difficulty in asking "Who is God?" is not *who* God is but how humanity perceives God. If there is a God that is all around us, how can that God ask us to attack one another over who is the best God? How can that be? Maybe it is not the thought of God who is attacking but the thoughts of men and women who perceive that their way of worship is the best, again going back to this religious nationalism in which the perception of being the strongest, mightiest, and most controlling is not about God but about power.

Who is God? God is faith. The rules and regulations that allow people to get along and not become animals—that is God. The hopes that one has in life—that is God. The thoughts and actions that allow humankind to live better—that is God. The perceptions that my God is better than your God—that is humanity.

If people of all faiths do not learn how to accept one another, it is not God's doing but human's.

Made in the USA
Lexington, KY
02 March 2017